GO

LONDON, NEW YORK,
MELBOURNE, MUNICH, AND DELHI

Written and edited by Samone Bos, Phil Hunt, Andrea Mills
Art Editors Joanne Little, Johnny Pau, Owen Peyton Jones, Stefan Podhorodecki, Samantha Richiardi, Jacqui Swan, Rebecca Wright

Senior Editors Julie Ferris, Sarah Larter
Senior Art Editor Smiljka Surla

Managing Editors Lin Esposito, Camilla Hallinan
Managing Art Editor Diane Thistlethwaite
Design Development Manager Sophia M Tampakopoulos Turner
Publishing Managers Caroline Buckingham, Andrew Macintyre
Category Publisher Laura Buller

Picture Researchers Marian Pullen, Frances Vargo
Production Controller Erica Rosen
DTP Designer Andy Hilliard
Jacket Designer Neal Cobourne
Jacket Editor Mariza O'Keeffe

Consultants Ian Graham, Henry Hope-Frost, Brian Lavery, Chris Sidwells, Hugo Wilson, Christian Wolmar
Additional text by Clare Hibbert

First published in Great Britain in 2006 by
Dorling Kindersley Limited,
80 Strand, London, WC2R 0RL

This edition produced for The Book People Ltd,
Hall Wood Avenue, Haydock, St Helens, WA11 9UL

Copyright © 2006 Dorling Kindersley Limited
A Penguin Company

2 4 6 8 10 9 7 5 3 1
GD054 – 06/06

A CIP catalogue record for this book is available from the British Library

ISBN-13: 978-1-40531-344-5
ISBN-10: 1-4053-1344-7

Colour reproduction by Colourscan, Singapore
Printed and bound by Hung Hing, China

Discover more at
www.dk.com

Contents

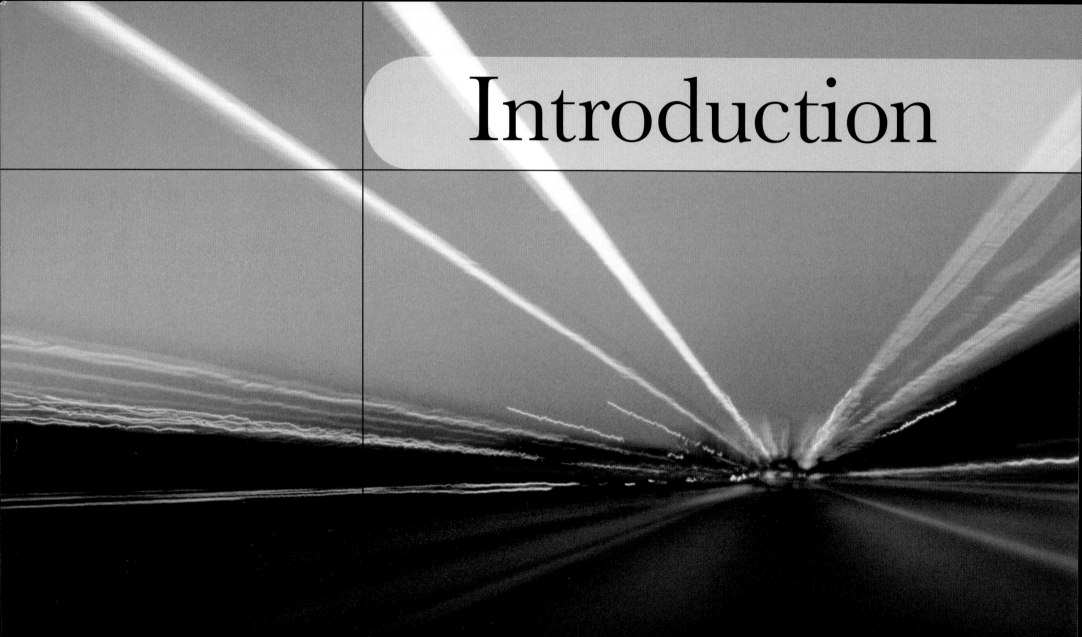

Introduction

Our lives are a series of journeys. They can be short walks or long-haul flights, taxi rides or a holiday cruise – as technology and innovation transform transportation by air, land, and water, never before have we gone so far so fast.

GO! takes us on a trail-blazing visual journey. It is an eye-popping exploration of the world of travel, from the ordinary to the extraordinary. Without taking a step, we will shoot over land on a bullet train, zip across the skies in a giant Airbus, sail the seas in a sleek superyacht, and leap from a plane with just a parachute. In three thematic chapters devoted to water, land, and air, *GO!* lifts the lid on the ways that people travel from A to B. We visit transport hubs all around the world and get first-hand accounts from passengers and workers. We peel back the roof of a jumbo jet, and pull apart all types of transport, from a classic car to a racing sailboat. Along the way, we witness hair-raising motocross stunts, glimpse a speeding rocket-powered car, and peer into airline sick bags. Our fascinating journey spans all five continents, going as far back as the first human footprint and as far forward as space tourism. Just where will we go next?

Water

Timeline

EARLY RAFT BOAT

First record of rafts
Migrants travelling from Southeast Asia reach Australia on rafts made of logs and reeds. This is the first record of rafts being used, and the migrants are Australia's first inhabitants.

GREEK VASE ENGRAVING

Greek warships
Galleys – large, shallow ships with sails and oars – are used as warships by the Greeks. They customize the design by adding a battering ram to smash enemy vessels.

BOW OF LONGBOAT

Viking longboats
The sight of distinctive Scandinavian longboats fills the people of northern Europe with fear. The Vikings launch raids from Scandinavia every summer in these vessels. Longboats carry armed warriors and their horses, and move easily in open sea and shallow rivers.

DISCOVERY OF NEW FOODS

Global exploration
Explorers use sailing ships to discover new lands. When Christopher Columbus leads an expedition across the Atlantic, he also finds new produce such as potatoes and tomatoes.

BRITISH 70-GUN TWO DECKER

Men-of-war
Sailing ships become fast and effective floating fortresses. European navies compete with each other by building heavily armed fighting ships called "men-of-war".

| c. 5000 BCE | c. 1000 BCE | 800 CE | 1492 | 1650 |
| c. 3100 BCE | c. 1 CE | 1200 | 1600 | 1661 |

Sail technology
Ancient Egyptians build sailing boats for fishing and transporting goods. They are the first people to use sails. This depiction of a sail painted on a vase is the first recorded use of a sail. The rectangular sails speed up travel along the slow-moving River Nile, but oars are still used to steer the boats.

VASE PAINTING OF EGYPTIAN SAIL BOAT

ROMAN COIN SHOWING GALLEY

Warring galleys
The Romans reinforce the sterns of the basic galley design for greater defence in sea battles. The galley is now the fastest vessel at sea. Galleys are used in war in ancient Persia, Greece, and Rome right up until the 16th century.

Chinese junks
The South China Sea suffers typhoons, so the Chinese junk is designed with a very strong, rigid hull. Junk is Malayan for "boat".

MODEL OF CHINESE JUNK

MODEL GALLEON

Racing galleon
English slave-trader John Hawkins improves the basic Spanish galleon design. Known as the "race-built" galleon, the new vessel is lower in the water and much faster.

PAINTING OF FIRST YACHT RACE

Yacht race
The first recorded yacht race takes place along the River Thames in London, England. Two royal ships take part in the race – King Charles II's *Catherine* and the Duke of York's *Anna*. Following this grand occasion, yachting regattas grow in popularity.

STATUE OF CAPTAIN COOK

Introduction of steamboats
US engineer Robert Fulton invents the first steamboat. Called *Clermont*, the vessel successfully travels from New York City to Albany in the USA. The vessel is the first ever to be fitted with paddle wheels instead of sails.

PAINTING OF CLERMONT

PROPELLER FROM THE MAURETANIA

Battleship development
Sea warfare is revolutionized by the development of battleships. These enormous vessels combine armour plating, steam propulsion, and guns. The gun turret is specially designed to fire shells over huge distances.

CROSS-SECTION OF A BATTLESHIP

Transatlantic containers
Despite the huge increase in air travel, 95 per cent of goods are still transported by sea. The American SeaLand line begins containerized shipping between the USA and Europe. Identical boxes are piled up on board so the ship can carry a greater load.

MAERSK SEALAND CONTAINER SHIP

Voyage of discovery
On board his ship *Endeavour*, English explorer Captain James Cook sails more than 48,000 km (29,800 miles) on a three-year voyage of exploration, during which he charts New Zealand.

Propellers
The propeller is invented to replace paddles. It is more efficient and able to work better in choppy seas. Due to the propeller's position on a ship, it is less likely to be damaged in a collision with another vessel.

▲ 1768   ▲ 1807   ▲ 1850   ▲ c. 1900   ▲ 1966

1790 ▼   1848 ▼   1898 ▼   c. 1960 ▼   2004 ▼

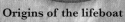

RESCUE LIFEBELT

Gold rush!
When gold is discovered in California, USA, prospectors travel from the east coast and around the tip of South America to reach California in the west. Fast clipper ships, with their multiple masts and sails, transport the fortune seekers.

PANNING FOR GOLD

Prototype submarine
John Philip Holland devises a submarine prototype. His designs prove a success and are adopted by the navies of Britain, Japan, Russia, Germany, and Sweden. He is hailed as "the father of the modern submarine".

JOHN PHILIP HOLLAND

QUEEN MARY 2

Super ships
Ships increase in size, scale, and luxury as tourists enjoy round-the-world cruises with more facilities and ports of call. The largest liner in the world is the *Queen Mary 2*.

Origins of the lifeboat
The first vessel specifically built to function as a lifeboat is constructed by Englishman Henry Greathead. Called *The Original*, it is launched on the River Tyne in England in 1790. The lifeboat makes its first rescue during the same year.

Pleasure craft
Sailing the seas becomes a leisure pursuit for many people and, to cope with the demand, varied types of pleasure boats and yachts are mass-produced. Racing yachts are constructed for use in competitions, and surfing takes off in the USA.

MODEL OF MOTORIZED YACHT

Ocean transporters

For thousands of years, boats and ships have transported people and goods all around the world. Their cargoes vary from fruit and fish to jeans and shoes; some may carry cars or aircraft parts, and others take passengers. For people living on remote islands, boats are often the only transport link with the outside world. Whether powered by oar, sail, steam, or diesel engine, these ocean transporters are vital to people's lives and livelihoods.

Junk
The Chinese perfected the junk design about 1,000 years ago. It has multiple masts, concertina sails, and a hull of watertight compartments. Merchant junks carried ceramics and silks to India, Arabia, and East Africa. Junks also engaged in sea battles and voyages of discovery, but now they are mostly used as family homes.

Sea barge
Designed for extremely heavy cargoes, a sea barge has the same capacity as 38 loaded river barges. Typical cargoes are dry bulk, such as coal or grain, and liquids, such as water or petrol. Military barges carry tanks or landing craft.

Dhow
Arab traders have used dhows to transport fruit, fish, and timber around the Indian Ocean for more than 2,000 years. Traditionally, the lateen (triangular) sails were made from palm leaves and the hull planks were stitched together with cord.

Hydrofoil
Built for speed and stability, a hydrofoil has a pair of wings or foils under the hull. As it accelerates, its hull lifts out of the water until only the foils are submerged. Hydrofoils have been used as passenger and car ferries since the 1950s.

Merchant ships

A merchant ship carries cargo from port to port. Smaller ships often service hub ports, where their cargoes are transferred to large container ships. They transport food, books, clothes, and electrical goods.

Naval ships

A variety of military ships are used for a range of missions. Some transport troops or essential supplies, while others patrol coastlines or drop touch-sensitive bombs called mines. Destroyers are among the most heavily armed warships in use today.

Outrigger canoe

Similar to stabilizers on a bicycle, outriggers are long floats that fix to each side of a boat and make it less likely to capsize. Outrigger canoes carried the first people to Polynesia from Southeast Asia about 5,000 years ago. Pacific islanders still use them for sea fishing.

Lepa

The Bajau people of Southeast Asia traditionally lived on wooden boats called lepa. They travelled from coast to coast, fishing and trading. Most Bajau have settled ashore now, but they continue to fish in their lepa. Many also take part in the annual lepa regatta at Semporna, Malaysia.

Basket boat

In Vietnam, fishermen paddle small basket boats. The boats are woven from thin strips of bamboo and have a waterproof, varnish coating. As well as being used for fishing, basket boats taxi tourists around the islands.

Superstitious sailors
In the face of uncontrollable weather and seas, it is no surprise that the sailing profession is so superstitious. The much-feared "evil eye", a talisman meant to deter the evil eye, dating back to 3000 BCE. According to some, black boats are meant to deter the evil eye, dating back to 3000 BCE. According to folklore, one glance from a person who unknowingly has an evil eye can bring bad luck, disease, and death. Sailors also believe green boats, red hair, black travelling bags, and horseshoes are lucky on a Friday bring bad luck. Mediterranean first referred to in texts dating back to 3000 BCE. According to folklore, bad luck, disease are lucky on a Friday bring bad luck. cats, rainbows, travelling bags, and horseshoes are lucky on a Friday bring bad luck. red hair, black travelling bags, black.

All in the name
Boat owners give a lot of thought to naming their vessels – a tradition Boat owners give the Ancient Egyptians named, almost all of them are. The started by the Ancient Egyptians named, almost all of them are. It is also laws exist requiring boats to be named, *Sea Spirit*, and *Escapade*. It is also laws exist requiring include *Serenity*, *Sea Spirit*, afer female family most popular names to name their vessels afer female family most popular boat owners to name their vessels the old name must common for boat owners to name their date is essential, the old name must common. Renaming the boat at a later date is essential, the old name must members. Renaming and best avoided. If renaming is erasing charts and log books. unlucky and best everything, including shipping charts and log books. be erased from everything, including shipping charts and log books.

Shipping identity

Sailors must depend on their vessels sometimes for their lives – and this often forges a strong attachment. They personalize their boats by giving them names, protect them with lucky talismans, and adorn them with flags, carvings, and decorations. Every boat has something that gives it its own individual identity.

Worn allegiance
Pride in a vessel and being part of a crew is integral to naval life, and wearing a uniform to show affiliation. Naval crews of different nations, as well as various classes of ships, adopt individual uniform's such as crew member's special features, and A higher-ranking crew adopt individual features, and can be identified by special stripes, and a double-breasted blazer, gold stripes, are worn peaked cap. Shoulder patches are worn to represent a variety of achievements.

Flying the flag
Whether displaying country of origin, or an individual insignia, flags are a common sight on every type of class of ship, hoist up national while Naval ships leaving harbour; while vessel and flags from on entering fly their battle flags submarines rig the conning tower before submerging. Smaller yachts and boats sometimes flags for decoration and miniature flags to indicate wind direction. up brightly coloured

Writing on the wall
When sailors dock in some Mediterranean ports, such as Funchal Harbour in Madeira, they paint pictures of their boats on the huge sea walls surrounding the harbours, including personal elements such as the names and on-board decorations that distinguish the boats. According to these harbours must draw their superstition, all sailors entering boats or add their vessel names to the walls to make sure they return to their home ports safely.

Container ship

Containerization has transformed cargo shipping, making it much easier and quicker to carry goods across the seas. Before the 1950s, loading and unloading ships was slow and laborious due to the different sizes and shapes of the cargo. Huge container ships now hold goods in standardized steel boxes that pile up perfectly like building blocks. Nicknamed "box boats", these ships transport at least 200 million containers every year.

The largest ships can carry more than 4,000 containers in one journey. Today, about 90 per cent of the world's dry cargo travels on board container ships.

■ The world's largest container ship is MSC *Pamela*, built by Samsung Heavy Industries in 2005. The vessel is 321 m (1,053 ft) long and 45 m (150 ft) wide. If the containers were lined up end to end, they would span 56 km (35 miles).

■ Pirates still attack ships, especially in the South China Sea, the Straits of Malacca, and off the coast of Brazil.

■ The busiest container ports are Singapore, Hong Kong in China, and Rotterdam in the Netherlands.

■ There are more than 350 container ships currently carrying passengers around the world. This figure is larger than the number of cruise ships in operation.

■ Cargo is stored on board in standard-length containers of 6 m (20 ft) and 12 m (40 ft).

■ The fuel burned by container ships is called "bunker 380". It has the consistency of tar and must be kept heated at all times to stop it turning into a solid lump in the fuel tank.

■ A container ship carrying 1,600 containers burns about 40 tonnes of fuel every day.

- Meat and fish are carried in temperature-controlled containers, known as "reefer containers", which have a refrigerator unit attached to one end.

- The average speed of a container ship is 32 kph (20 mph). During the course of 24 hours, a container ship will travel on average 800 km (497 miles).

- The Brazilian wandering spider is known as the "banana spider" because some have been found on container ships carrying bananas to the USA.

- The bestselling novel Roots was written on a container ship. Author Alex Haley was inspired by the peace and solitude.

- Rain and seawater is drained away through a "scupper" – a tiny hole located on the top deck of a container ship.

- Container ships must be loaded with care as improperly stored cargo makes a vessel unstable, particularly in stormy seas.

- Each container is anchored by "twist locks", which twist to lock the eight corners of the container to the container next to it.

- Every year, about 10,000 containers fall from ships and land in the sea. Storms are usually the cause of this.

- In 2002, the Norwegian Tricolor was carrying £30 million (US$55 million) worth of luxury cars when it sank after a collision.

- Most container ships have a crew of 30 people. The accommodation area is located at the stern, above the engine room.

- In 1992, several containers on a ship bound for the USA fell overboard. As a result, about 29,000 plastic bath toys were left floating in the sea!

- American Malcolm McLean invented the concept of shipping containers in the 1930s.

- The first container ships were converted tankers, adapted after World War II.

Ship shape

Today's high-tech shipbuilding is a far cry from the art of the ancient shipwright, who spent months seasoning timber, nailing hull planks, and stitching sails. Steel and state-of-the-art plastics have replaced wood, computers now assist with the design, cutting is carried out by robots, and cranes heave enormous prefabricated sections of the vessels into place. The biggest modern shipyards are in Asia, where land and labour are inexpensive. This is also where ships go to be broken up.

Hull construction
In a fountain of sparks, a construction worker welds steel plates onto the bulkhead of HMS *Tyne*, a warship. Protective overalls, gloves, and goggles are essential for this dangerous work. Welding has been commonplace since World War II. Before then, the steel plates were fastened together with metal rivets.

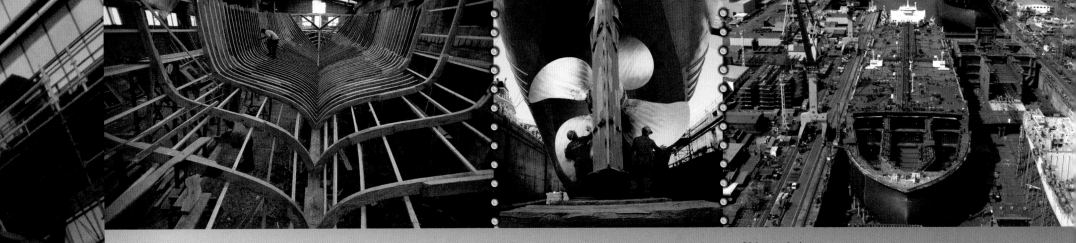

Working with wood

This Turkish shipwright is working on a rib of a traditional wooden fishing vessel called a *çektirme*. Until the 19th century, most ships were built from timber using one of two methods of construction: the first was to create a wooden skeleton, then nail on the hull planks. The second involved making the hull shell first, adding an internal framework later.

Dry dock

Hundreds of people are involved in the building of a ship, including engineers, welders, plumbers, electricians, painters, and carpenters. Construction often takes place in a dry dock to give workers complete access to the vessel. Wooden supports called stocks hold the ship in place.

Shipyard site

One of the world's largest shipyards is Daewoo in South Korea. China, Japan, and South Korea lead the way in shipbuilding and have huge steel industries to supply the raw materials. Shipyards sprawl along the coastlines, employing tens of thousands of people. Some produce as many as 70 large vessels every year.

Ship launch

Whether large or small, new ships are named prior to launch. The crude oil carrier NS *Challenger* was named at a special ceremony in January 2005. If the ship is on land, it is towed down a ramp into the sea. More often, the ship is in dry dock. This fills with water and the vessel is launched.

Regular maintenance

After launch, a vessel must still return to dry dock at various times during its life. Ships are regularly checked, repaired, and modified to ensure they stay safe and seaworthy. Workers here are cleaning an anchor to minimize the build-up of rust.

End of the liner

Once a vessel is old and unseaworthy, it is broken up for scrap and recycling. Most ships are dismantled at Chittagong in Bangladesh or Alang in India. Steel plates, machinery, and even toilets are salvaged. Crews work with little more than their bare hands, so accidents are common.

Oil!

Without oil, many of the journeys we make would not be possible. Powering our cars, boats, and planes, this fossil fuel is integral to our lives. Oil forms from the remnants of minute animals and plants that died in the world's oceans millions of years ago. As a result, oil is often found in remote parts of the seabed and must make a long journey of its own in order to become all the varied and useful products we recognize today.

Huge oil tankers, known as crude carrier tankers, carry 62 per cent of the crude oil found at sea to refineries around the world. About 3,500 tankers are currently used to transport oil.

Knock Nevis, the world's biggest oil tanker

Oil production platform in the North Sea

On offshore oil platforms, workers use huge drills to dig deep down into the seabed for oil. An undersea pipe connects the platform to a loading rig, which fills either a tanker or a pipe with oil.

An underwater pipeline in the North Sea

About 38 per cent of the world's oil is carried by undersea pipelines. Although pipelines are invaluable once built, they are generally very costly and complicated to lay under the sea.

Oil refinery in Montreal, Canada

Oil is transported to a refinery, an industrial plant where the impurities in crude oil are removed. The purified substance is distilled and undergoes other separation and refinement processes before it is turned into a range of by-products.

The variety of by-products are taken by tanker for delivery around the world. The tankers are enormous, often more than 450 m (1,475 ft) long, 60 m (195 ft) wide, and 25 m (80 ft) deep. Due to their size, tankers are hard to steer and it can take 15 minutes to bring one to a halt. Some crews cycle around the decks to save time.

Anchored tanker preparing to make a delivery of oil by-products

In 2005, 1.9 billion tonnes of crude oil were shipped around the world. The scale of this demand comes from the diverse range of products derived from crude oil. Apart from fuel for transport, the end-products of oil are all around us, in paraffin, plastics, synthetics, rubber, waxes, and lubricants. From insecticides to perfumes, asphalt to detergents, and crayons to tyres, oil proves a versatile, invaluable resource.

Aviation fuel and petrol are two of the major uses of refined oil.

A section of the Trans-Alaska pipeline system

If a destination is landlocked, has a short coastline, or the distance to travel is reduced by taking a land route, then pipelines are used to transport the oil by-products instead of tankers. The pipes are usually above ground. If the area is built-up or protected by conservation legislation, the pipes are laid 1 m (3 ft) underground.

A series of pump stations lining the horizontal pipes keep the oil by-products moving quickly to their destination. Without the pumps the liquid and gas products inside would be unable to flow along the pipes.

Tanker offloading oil products in California

Pipelines link up to docks and cities where the by-products can be deposited. Similarly, tankers dock and deposit their by-products at ports all over the world. A system called Worldscale now regulates tankers. This ensures tankers carry products worldwide, and not just to affluent countries. Tanker owners earn a fixed rate regardless of the length or difficulty of the trip. On arrival, products are stored in containers, and trains or trucks are used to distribute them.

Oil facts and figures

- One barrel of oil is the same as 159 litres (35 gallons), which is enough to fill the petrol tanks of four standard cars.
- The UK uses almost 2 million barrels of oil every single day.
- The world's largest oil field is in Saudi Arabia. It is 70 km (43 miles) long and 30 km (19 miles) wide.
- In 1877, the first oil tanker, the steam-powered *Zoroaster*, was built to transport kerosene in the Caspian sea.
- One of the largest oil pipelines is the Trans-Alaska pipeline system. It is 1,300 km (807 miles) long, and crosses three mountain ranges as well as 800 rivers and streams.
- The oil drill bit has industrial diamonds on the cutting edges. Diamonds are hard enough to cut through rock.
- In 1989, the *Exxon Valdez* tanker ran aground in Alaska, spilling 11 million barrels of oil. The clean-up cost for the first year was £1.4 billion ($2 billion).

Linking oceans

The Panama Canal is an artificial waterway connecting the Atlantic and Pacific oceans in Central America. Although its construction was one of the most difficult engineering projects in history, the end result has transformed the world's shipping routes for the better. No longer do ships need to travel the lengthy and dangerous path around Cape Horn at the southern tip of South America; instead, they can cut straight through the narrow strip of Panama. More than 850,000 vessels have used the canal since its completion in 1914.

Canal path

The Panama Canal spans 82 km (51 miles). It cuts through the country of Panama, connecting the Pacific Ocean with the Caribbean Sea and on to the Atlantic Ocean.

Caribbean Sea

PACIFIC OCEAN

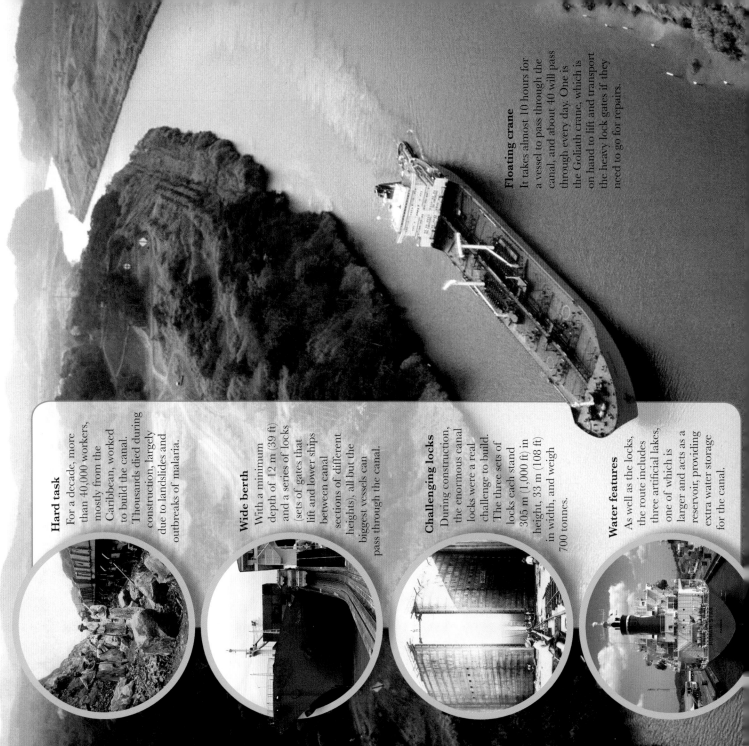

Floating crane

It takes almost 10 hours for a vessel to pass through the canal, and about 40 will pass through every day. One is the Goliath crane, which is on hand to lift and transport the heavy lock gates if they need to go for repairs.

Hard task

For a decade, more than 40,000 workers, mostly from the Caribbean, worked to build the canal. Thousands died during construction, largely due to landslides and outbreaks of malaria.

Wide berth

With a minimum depth of 12 m (39 ft) and a series of locks (sets of gates that lift and lower ships between canal sections of different heights), all but the biggest vessels can pass through the canal.

Challenging locks

During construction, the enormous canal locks were a real challenge to build. The three sets of locks each stand 305 m (1,000 ft) in height, 33 m (108 ft) in width, and weigh 700 tonnes.

Water features

As well as the locks, the route includes three artificial lakes, one of which is larger and acts as a reservoir, providing extra water storage for the canal.

Cutting continents

Built to provide the fastest crossing from the Atlantic Ocean to the Indian Ocean, the Suez is one of the world's largest canals and connects the Mediterranean Sea to the Gulf of Suez. Completed in 1869, this huge achievement was a combined effort by French and British engineers. Today, the Suez carries 14 per cent of world shipping.

Super size
Unlike the Panama, the simpler Suez has no locks so almost any size and type of ship can pass through, including oil platforms.

Canal path
The Suez is 190 km (118 miles) long, with a minimum width of 60 m (197 ft). Ships can travel from Europe to Asia without circumnavigating Africa.

Single file
Most of the Suez Canal has room for only one lane of traffic. However, passing bays are scattered along the route.

Suez from space
The Suez Canal is so large that it can be clearly seen from space. Here, the Great Bitter Lake is visible at the canal's centre.

Ports of call

Chennai, India
During the 1600s, the English East India Company began to trade from the fishing village of Chennai, in southeastern India. The fishing industry is still thriving today, but Chennai's three artificial harbours also handle more than 35 million tonnes of international cargo a year.

Hong Kong, China
With its huge, sheltered natural harbour, Hong Kong is one of the world's busiest container ports. Around 220,000 vessels dock here each year. As well as container ships, there are passenger ferries, cruise liners, and oil tankers. Every June, the port hosts the city's famous dragon boat races.

CONTAINER PORTS
These ports cover a large area as the enormous container ships need room to dock. The equipment used to pack the goods on board and send them on to their final destinations also requires a vast expanse of space. Hong Kong, Shanghai, and Singapore are among the world's busiest container ports.

Most of the world's major cities are served by a port with commercial facilities where ships and boats can dock. Ports often bustle with activity as boats arrive and depart, cranes unload container ships, and workers busy themselves in local warehouses. A network of transport links, such as railways, roads, and rivers carries goods inland. Similar to ports, harbours shelter boats from the sea. Natural harbours are enclosed by land, while artificial ones have sea walls. Harbours with special moorings for yachts are called marinas.

Rotterdam, The Netherlands

Europe's busiest port is Rotterdam. It is built around the Nieuwe Maas, a river connecting the Rhine and the North Sea. Crude oil, iron ore, and coal make up almost half of Rotterdam's cargo, and there are five oil refineries in the industrial area around the port.

Depoe Bay, Oregon, USA

The port of Depoe Bay on the Pacific coast is considered to be the world's smallest navigable harbour. The bay is landlocked, except for one small entrance through the tough basalt rocks that form the sides of the harbour. Fishing boats bring in salmon, halibut, and flounder, while charter vessels take people whale-watching.

Auckland, New Zealand

Known as the "City of Sails", Auckland has hosted two America's Cup challenges. It has two harbours – Waitemata on the Pacific and Manukau on the Tasman Sea. Both are packed with yachts. In 2005, the first Auckland Harbour Festival took place, with tall ships races, yacht regattas, and fireworks.

FISHING PORTS

Every year, ships bring about 85 million tonnes of fish, shellfish, and molluscs into the world's fishing ports. Tuna is the main deep-sea catch. Most ports have a fish market, with Tokyo in Japan being one of the world's biggest. Many ports also have canning factories or processing plants.

RIVER PORTS

Not all ports are directly by the sea or ocean. They can also be situated on rivers, canals, or lakes. The port of Kampala, the capital of Uganda, lies on Lake Victoria. Some river ports, such as Rotterdam in the Netherlands, have links to the ocean along deep waterways.

MINI-PORTS

Some harbours are so tiny that boats cannot even move around in them. The Italian island of Ginostra, for example, has a harbour that is just 3 m (10 ft) wide. Once inside, fishing boats have to be hauled on to a paved slope to make way for other incoming vessels.

PLEASURE PORTS

Ports around the Caribbean are very popular with yachtspeople because of the region's fine weather and good sailing conditions. There are 30 marinas in the Bahamas alone. Europe's most famous pleasure port is Monte Carlo, Monaco, on the Mediterranean coast.

The passengers

Every day, an eclectic mix of people use the Sydney Ferries. Visitors from all over the world come to see the sights and enjoy the surrounding bays, commuters regularly catch boats to work, and locals find the vessels ideal for day trips.

Mac

Every morning, fisherman Mac returns with his catch for the market. "Fishing is really hard work. We do long hours and it gets very tiring," he explains.

Erin and Michael

On holiday from Melbourne, Erin and Michael enjoy the ferry tours. "The ferry is less stressful than car traffic," says Michael.

Vincent

For 20 years, Parisian pastry chef Vincent has caught the first ferry at 5.40 am. "I grab a coffee, sit down, and admire the view."

Hilary

Hilary always chooses a window seat for her ferry commute to work. "I love the traditional, friendly ferries. They are the calmest way to travel."

John

With his passion for boats, John enjoys sightseeing tours by ferry. "The best time to go on a tour is at night when the city is all lit up."

Nicole

Californian student Nicole is visiting Sydney. "The ferries are cheap, easy to ride, and ideal for visiting different, picturesque places."

Travelling on water

Commuters, locals, and tourists mingle at central Circular Quay where Sydney Ferries is based. From here, the ferries carry travellers to and from more than 40 wharves around the harbour at regular times throughout the day.

Harbour life

■ Established in 1788, Sydney Harbour was the first permanent European settlement in Australia.
■ In 2004, there were 4.3 million people living in Sydney and 2.6 million short-term visitors to the city from other countries.
■ Before the Sydney Harbour Bridge opened in 1932, 400 million passenger journeys were made on the ferries each year. Today, the ferries annually carry more than 14 million people around the city and the surrounding suburbs.
■ Circular Quay is the busiest transport hub in the whole of Sydney. As well as the ferry terminal, which has eight piers, it is also home to the city's main bus station and a train station linking the city centre with the southern and eastern suburbs.
■ The thriving surfer's beach and café town of Manly is the most popular destination for ferry passengers.

Sydney Harbour ferries

Sydney is one of the most beautiful maritime cities in the world. With its deep waters, coves, and inlets, it is Australia's busiest port. The harbour throngs with cargo ships carrying millions of tonnes of imports and exports, luxury liners docking for a stay in the city, pleasure cruisers soaking up the scenery, and fishermen landing catches from the Pacific Ocean. Every day, the harbour ferries carry commuters to work and take tourists to see the iconic landmarks.

Sydney Harbour
One of the largest natural harbours in the world, Sydney Harbour stretches 19 km (12 miles) and covers an area of 55 sq km (34 sq miles). The famous steel arch bridge connects the north and south of the city.

The workers

The running of Sydney Ferries Corporation is a real team effort. From the skippers steering the vessels to the deck hands and ticket sellers, the crew support each other in order to meet the demands of the busy ferry timetable.

Michael H

As part of Customer Services, Michael helps visiting tourists make best use of the ferries. "We suggest the most interesting routes."

John

Ferry engineer John maintains the boats. "I start the engines in the morning, check them throughout the day, and shut them down at night."

Gregory

Heading up a team of three, Greg is responsible for controlling ferry movements. "We have a million dollar view working here," he says.

Michael B

Passenger care and docking ferries are deck hand Michael's concerns. "The best thing about my job is getting paid to be at Sydney Harbour."

Nada

Nada sells the ferry tickets to customers at the harbour kiosk. "We do three 12-hour shifts in a row so I drink a lot of coffee!"

Kris

There are about 80 captains working on Sydney Ferries and Kris is one of them. As skipper, he steers and navigates the vessel. He explains, "I started here as a deck hand and that was over 30 years ago!"

Fleet of ferries

■ Sydney Ferries have cruised around Sydney Harbour for more than 135 years.
■ The fleet consists of 31 vessels divided into seven classes. Each class of ferry carries a different number of passengers.

■ The largest class of ferry is the distinctive green and yellow Freshwater. There are four of these and each carries up to 1,100 passengers.
■ The smallest class of ferry is called RiverCat.

There are seven in the fleet, each carrying 230 passengers.
■ The fleet of ferries operates approximately 110,000 trips each year and annually travels about 1.3 million km (807,300 miles).

■ The network stretches 37 km (23 miles), with central Sydney at its core. It includes the nearby suburb of Parramatta in the west, the seaside resort of Manly in the northeast, and the fishing village of Watson's Bay in the east.

Water rescue

The ocean is a dangerous place with strong currents, shifting sea beds, and unpredictable weather. Rescue services are trained to respond to any emergency call-out and include large lifeboats, small inflatable craft, helicopters, individual lifeguards, and even dogs. They must go to the assistance of a swimmer swept out to sea, a diver drifting in shark-infested waters, a fishing boat lashed by strong seas, or an oil tanker breaking up on rocks. In the Arctic Sea, ice-breaker vessels cut a path through the ice to help container ships get past. In warmer parts of the world, the crews of boats caught up in tropical storms may need assistance. All around the world, many people owe their lives to these brave rescue teams.

Rescue records

■ Englishmen William Wouldhave (1751–1821) and Lionel Lukin (1742–1834) both claimed to have invented the lifeboat.

■ The first lifeboat was tested on the River Tyne in England on 29 January 1790.

■ The longest time adrift at sea was 484 days. Oguri Jukichi from Japan was stuck at sea when his ship was damaged in a storm. From October 1813, he drifted off the Japanese coast until he was finally rescued by a US ship off California on 24 March 1815.

■ The longest journey in a lifeboat was completed when Sir Ernest Shackleton took a small lifeboat called *James Caird* from Elephant Island to South Georgia. The distance covered was 1,287 km (800 miles).

■ When the ocean liner *Titanic* hit an iceberg and sank in 1912, it had only 20 lifeboats on board, capable of carrying just 52 per cent of the passengers.

■ The largest totally enclosed lifeboat, known as a TELB, is the Norwegian Norsafe. It can carry 90 people and the cover protects against fire and toxic gases.

Modern lifeboats

Lifeboats are designed to be self-righting, which means they roll back to be the right way up if they capsize. The boats rely on Global Positioning Systems (GPS) and radar for navigation. They carry fire extinguishers, life buoys, distress flares, and pumps to remove water from sinking ships. First-aid kits, breathing equipment, blankets, and food and drink are kept on board to treat survivors. The captain radios to shore if the lifeboat needs to be met by an ambulance.

Inflatable assistance

Most inshore life rafts are rigid inflatables with room for five people. If many survivors need to be picked up at once, such as after a plane crash, large inflatable platforms are used. These can be dropped from the air or thrown from a lifeboat or life raft.

Helicopter rescue

Helicopters airlift people to safety from the sea or drop life-jackets to keep people afloat until a lifeboat arrives. They also bring search-and-rescue dogs to the scene that can detect people underwater. This dog is being trained to swim out to a victim.

Solo savers

In Australia, beachside water rescues are performed by individual lifeguards. Each lifeguard has a rescue surfboard, which doubles up as a stretcher, a rescue tube to tow survivors back to shore, and a pair of flippers to help swim quickly to an emergency.

Underwater world

With more than two-thirds of the Earth's surface covered in ocean, it is no wonder that people are keen to explore it. Pioneering designs and developments in the form of apparatus, vehicles, and vessels are opening up our oceans as never before. From the sparkling surface to the darkest depths, people can now view marine creatures, salvage wrecks, study water life, and monitor oil platforms.

① Glassbottom boat

Boats with sections of glass below the waterline enable passengers to view the marine world without even getting wet. Issues such as safety and use of breathing apparatus do not matter as tourists sit back and enjoy the on-board comforts. These trips are popular in clear, warm waters where marine life flourishes and tourists are guaranteed sightings of underwater creatures and plants.

② Snuba

This is a hybrid form of snorkelling and scuba diving. Divers use standard scuba breathing apparatus, but the compressed air tanks are located on floating rafts at the water's surface. The air reaches the divers through a long, thin hose. Snuba divers can also use motorized engines to travel around the shallow waters.

③ Seawalking

Underwater helmets are all that is needed for a walk along the sea bed. The Underwater Helmet Diving System is an innovative invention allowing the amount of air necessary for normal breathing to be delivered to the helmet. Air circulates within the weighted helmet and the diver breathes as normal. Seawalking is most common in the warm waters of the southern hemisphere.

④ Hydropolis hotel

The world's first underwater hotel is currently being built 20 m (66 ft) beneath the surface of the Arabian Gulf in Dubai.

Held in place by 7,000 anchors, Hydropolis consists of a land station where guests arrive, a connecting tunnel to transport people to the main hotel block, and 220 underwater suites.

The hotel is expected to cost £300 million (US$549 million) to build.

Sea level
0 m
(0 ft)

6 m
(20 ft)

20 m
(66 ft)

50 m
(164 ft)

209 m
(686 ft)

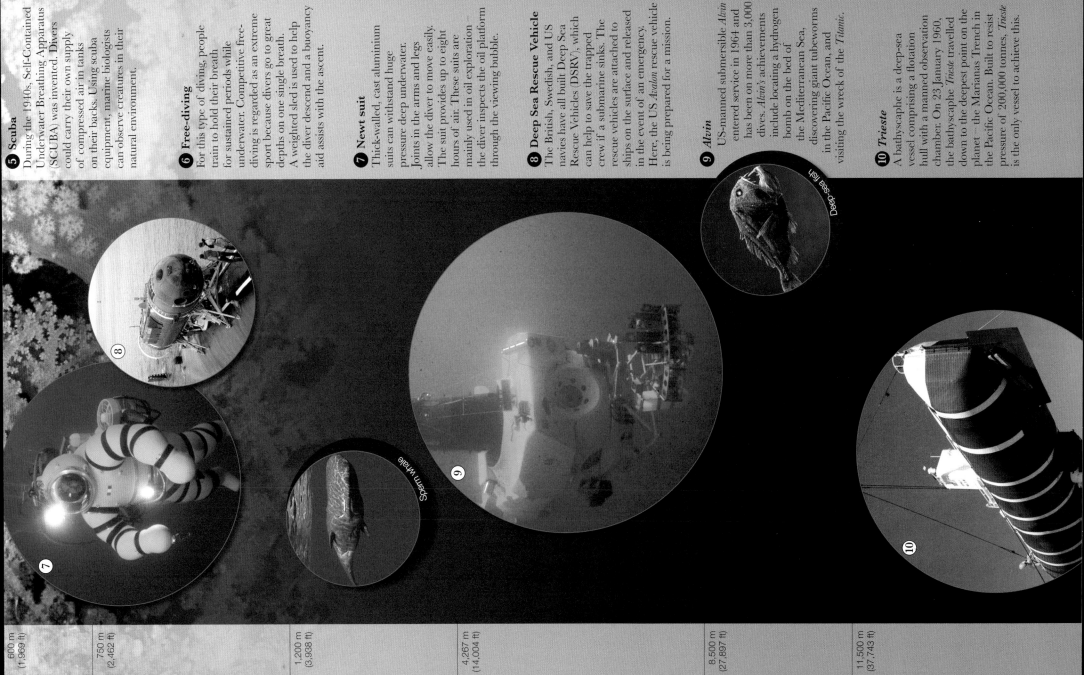

5 Scuba

During the 1940s, Self-Contained Underwater Breathing Apparatus (SCUBA) was invented. Divers could carry their own supply of compressed air in tanks on their backs. Using scuba equipment, marine biologists can observe creatures in their natural environment.

6 Free-diving

For this type of diving, people train to hold their breath for sustained periods while underwater. Competitive free-diving is regarded as an extreme sport because divers go to great depths on one single breath. A weighted sled is used to help the diver descend and a buoyancy aid assists with the ascent.

7 Newt suit

Thick-walled, cast aluminium suits can withstand huge pressure deep underwater. Joints in the arms and legs allow the diver to move easily. The suit provides up to eight hours of air. These suits are mainly used in oil exploration – the diver inspects the oil platform through the viewing bubble.

8 Deep Sea Rescue Vehicle

The British, Swedish, and US navies have all built Deep Sea Rescue Vehicles (DSRV), which can help to save the trapped crew if a submarine sinks. The rescue vehicles are attached to ships on the surface and released in the event of an emergency. Here, the US *Avalon* rescue vehicle is being prepared for a mission.

9 *Alvin*

US-manned submersible *Alvin* entered service in 1964 and has been on more than 3,000 dives. *Alvin's* achievements include locating a hydrogen bomb on the bed of the Mediterranean Sea, discovering giant tubeworms in the Pacific Ocean, and visiting the wreck of the *Titanic*.

10 *Trieste*

A bathyscaphe is a deep-sea vessel comprising a flotation hull with a manned observation chamber. On 23 January 1960, the bathyscaphe *Trieste* travelled down to the deepest point on the planet – the Marianas Trench in the Pacific Ocean. Built to resist pressure of 200,000 tonnes, *Trieste* is the only vessel to achieve this.

Sperm whale

Deep-sea fish

600 m
(1,969 ft)

750 m
(2,462 ft)

1,200 m
(3,938 ft)

4,267 m
(14,004 ft)

8,500 m
(27,897 ft)

11,500 m
(37,743 ft)

Submarine

Nuclear-powered submarines can stay at sea for months at a time without resurfacing. The nuclear power provides an unlimited source of heat to turn water into steam, allowing submarines to travel long distances at high speed. This has revolutionized sea warfare, with nuclear submarines such as the US Navy's Seawolf-class able to reach depths of more than 600 m (1,970 ft) and travel around the world without refuelling. Today, the only limitation to time spent at sea is the food supply on board.

SEAWOLF (SSN-21) CLASS

This class of submarine is larger, faster, quieter, and more expensive than any submarine to date. For shallow-water missions, each vessel has a floodable chamber called a silo used to place eight divers and their equipment into water.

Specifications:

Length	108 m (354 ft)
Width	12 m (39 ft)
Speed	65 kph (40 mph)
Depth (min)	11 m (36 ft)
Depth (max)	600 m (1,970 ft)
Power	S6W nuclear reactor
Crew	133 (12 officers, 121 sailors)

Weapons room
In its double-deck weapons room, a Seawolf-class submarine is equipped to carry tomahawk cruise missiles, harpoon missiles, torpedoes, and mines. The torpedoes can be launched via one of the eight torpedo tubes on board. The well-equipped weapons room allows the submarine to respond to military threats from other submarines, ships, and even air attacks.

Driving force
The control room of a modern submarine resembles an aircraft's flight deck. The submarine "pilots" must control the angle and depth of the vessel to keep it straight and level. The submarine can manoeuvre at high speed and extreme angles, but restraining straps keep the crew safely in their seats.

Life on board
Ventilation, air purification systems, and a substantial fresh water supply for drinking and bathing are all features of modern submarines. The multi-deck Seawolf-class submarines offer more spacious sleeping quarters than smaller vessels, in which sailors sleep between racks of torpedoes. When off duty, submariners can play computer games and watch films.

Aircraft carrier

Aircraft carriers are among the world's largest ships, able to support a crew of more than 6,000. The Nimitz class of modern nuclear-powered super-carriers is the largest of all and includes the USS *George Washington*. Launched in 1990, the carrier is 333 m (1,093 ft) long, 78 m (256 ft) wide, and the same height as a 24-storey building. Although it could travel for 18 years without refuelling, most missions only last a few months.

Bridge The super-carrier is steered from a forward-facing bridge. Navigation facilities for the captain are also found here.

Operations room Staff constantly monitor live screen pictures of the comings and goings on the flight deck. They also use radar systems to survey the air space above the carrier.

Engine controls The carrier has two nuclear reactors, which are controlled remotely from this base.

Briefing room The pilots have meetings and debriefings in this room. There is a seat specifically for each pilot. The head-rest of every seat is marked with the call sign of an individual pilot.

Primary flight control The tricky takeoffs and landings are coordinated from this position overlooking the flight deck.

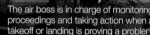

The air boss is in charge of monitoring proceedings and taking action when a takeoff or landing is proving a problem

Island superstructure This area is the central core of the carrier, housing the bridge, primary flight control centre, and air traffic control centre. The Island is decorated with awards for excellence.

Takeoff The runway is only 91 m (298 ft) long, so huge acceleration is needed to clear it. Planes must have a lot of air moving over the wings at takeoff. The carrier ploughs through water to increase the airflow catapults are used to speed planes u

Helicopter In case of an emergency, such as an aircraft falling over the side, the carrier's helicopters are on hand to assist.

Weapons The aircraft on board inclu fighter, strike, and transport planes. T carry a variety of weapons, such as

e carrier is powered for a year a piece of fuel the same size a drink can!

Pumping fuel In the pump room, fuel (known as "JP5") for the aircraft and other engines is filtered and pumped up to the flight deck. There is a laboratory on board where the JP5 fuel is regularly analyzed for consistency.

Bakery The chefs knead the dough before cooking it in the ovens. Each day, hundreds of loaves are freshly baked.

Canteen The enormous canteen caters for the crew of 6,000 men and women three times a day.

Gym A state-of-the-art gym is essential to ensure the crew stays fit enough to carry out the demanding on-board procedures.

ck crew The flight deck is patrolled by officers o use radio communication to help guide the nes around the carrier.

Catapult control This is a retractable pod where crew involved in the takeoff of aircraft can view the deck, while staying at a safe distance.

Catapult This is one of four steam-powered catapults, used to get planes to high speeds over a very short distance.

Preparing for takeoff A Hawkeye aircraft is secured to a catapult system that will project it quickly into the air.

Signalling takeoff When giving clearance for takeoff, crew members wear helmets called "cranials" to block out engine noise.

ing Every plane has a tailhook. To stop quickly, pilot must hook this on to one of four wires laid out the carrier deck.

Arresting An aircraft picks up one of four wires with its tailhook, and comes to an abrupt halt. This is called "arresting". If an aircraft misses the wires, the pilot takes off again and attempts another landing. This practice is called "touch and go".

mbs, rockets, guided missiles, d torpedoes. These are used air, sea, and land missions.

Propeller shaft A crewman checks a shaft driving one of the super-carrier's four giant propellers.

Maintenance In the engine-maintenance bay, aircraft undergo routine checks. If there is a serious technical problem, the aircraft is grounded until the fault is fixed.

Aircraft hangar When the carrier's 85 aircraft are not in use or on the flight deck, they are stored in the hangar. Servicing crews regularly check and maintain them. The hangar is three decks high and has four massive lifts to manoeuvre the planes and spare parts to and from the flight deck.

Mechanics of sailing

Dinghy sailing is a thrilling sport, but it requires training, skill, and determination. First, a sailor must understand how the boat works. A sailing boat harnesses the power of the wind in its sails and uses this to move in a particular direction. The boat's four main parts are the hull, keel, sails, and rudder. The hull is the body of the boat. It keeps the water out, holds the mast, and provides somewhere for the crew to sit. The keel is a beam that runs along the bottom of the hull and prevents the boat being blown sideways. There are usually two sails and these are attached to a mast. A sailor must fine-tune the position of the sails almost constantly, aiming to keep the wind flowing over them as smoothly as possible. The rudder is integral to steering the boat. It is a flat piece of material, such as wood or fibreglass, that projects from part of the stern (back) of the boat into the water. The rudder is moved left or right using a lever called a tiller. It does not take long to learn the parts of a boat and the basic principles of sailing, but it takes years to become an experienced sailor, ready to meet any challenge at sea.

Rigging and ropes

The mast is held up by a mesh of ropes known as rigging. There is a pole jutting out from the bottom of the mast to support the sail and this is called the boom. Rectangular sails have another pole, known as a yard, at the top. The ropes for adjusting the sails are called sheets. All the ropes tie on to fittings called cleats.

Points of sailing

Wind moving past a sail produces a force at right angles to the sail. Adjusting the sail takes the boat in different directions, known as the points of sailing. A sailing boat can travel in any direction except straight into the wind (the no-go zone). The only way around it is to take a zig-zag course – this is called tacking.

Mainsail

Batton

Mast

Rigging

8008

Boom

Stern

Hull

Rudder

Tiller

Gunwhales

Side deck

Cleat

Jib sail

Fore deck

Bow

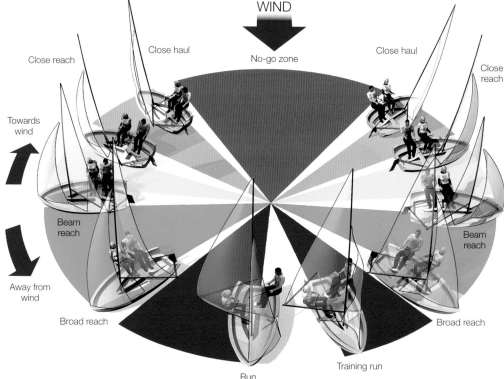

WIND

Close reach

Close haul

No-go zone

Close haul

Close reach

Towards wind

Beam reach

Beam reach

Away from wind

Broad reach

Broad reach

Training run

Run

Balancing the boat

Sailors can use their own bodies to counteract the force of the wind and keep the boat as upright in the water as possible. The sailing team consists of a helmsman, who makes key decisions and controls on-board procedures, together with a support crew of at least one person. The team on this racing dinghy are standing on the gunwhales – the top edge of the side of the boat. They lean out of the windward side, pulling against the billowing sails.

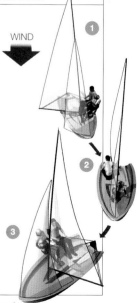

TACKING: SAILING TOWARDS THE WIND

Turning so that the bow (front) of the boat passes through the wind is called tacking. Taking a series of zig-zag turns allows the boat to reach a part of the no-go zone.

WIND

1 The helmsman and crew member sit forwards. The helmsman controls the mainsheet (rope to adjust the mainsail) and tiller. The crew member controls the jib sheet.

2 The helmsman calls "lee-oh!" and pushes the tiller towards the sail. The crew member releases the jib sheet. Both move to the centre. As the boat turns, the crew member lifts the other jib sheet to fill the sails.

3 The helmsman moves the tiller to central and trims the sails – this involves pulling on the sheets to adjust the sail positions. Both helmsman and crew member sit back to balance the boat.

GYBING: SAILING AWAY FROM THE WIND

Turning so that the stern (back) of the boat passes through the wind is called gybing. In strong winds, the turn is extremely quick, but in light winds, the boat turns through a slow, wide arc.

WIND

1 Gybing is a tricky manoeuvre. Before starting the turn, the helmsman checks that the boat is balanced, the area is clear, and the main sheet is hauled in tight.

2 The helmsman and crew member move to the boat's centre. The helmsman calls "gybe-oh!" and ducks as the boom starts to swing across the stern. As it reaches the centre, the helmsman centres the tiller.

3 The helmsman and crew member shift their weight to the new windward side of the boat. The crew member adjusts the jib sail, known as "trimming the jib".

Strong sails

The fabric of the RS700 sails is reinforced with the material Kevlar®, which is stronger than steel and prevents ripping or snagging. The spinnaker (balloon-like sail, forward of the mainsail) is protected by a water-repellent silicon coating. Kevlar® and silicon give the sails a much longer life at sea before they must be replaced.

Balancing act

In light winds, the RS700 stays flat with no danger of keeling over. When the wind picks up, the sailor must use his or her body weight to balance the boat. In strong winds, any skiff with large sails needs a trapeze to stay balanced. A trapeze is a rope connected to the mast, allowing the sailor to suspend him or herself out of the boat. This counteracts the effect of the wind while maintaining racing speed.

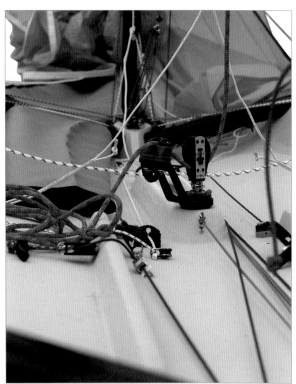

Racing sailboat

Ideal for solo sailing, the RS700 skiff (shallow boat) was designed with racing in mind. The size and weight of the sailor was previously a factor in racing – the lighter and smaller the sailor, the faster the boat powered through the waves. The RS700's performance equalization system eliminates this. Adjustable "wings" (beams attached to the hull) are extended or narrowed to ensure that all sailors have the same height advantage, and a lead track with weights makes the load of each boat identical. With the race fair, anyone can be a winner!

Fast moves

In a single-handed racing skiff, everything must be easy for the solo sailor to reach and operate. The simple design of the RS700 allows the sailor to take up a secure central position behind the mast and move freely around the boat. The ropes are clearly colour-coded, allowing the sailor to quickly identify which one operates the mainsail, spinnaker, or boom (sail support), without wasting time during a race.

Dry hull
The long, pointed shape of the hull (vessel frame) helps the RS700 to move faster in water. Although the hull weighs only 56 kg (123 lb), it is strong and stable. Very little seawater can enter the hull. If the boat goes through a wave, the open deck at the bow (front) is designed to shed any excess water quickly. This means race entrants can keep their speed up without surplus water slowing them down.

Built for speed

Boats competing in the America's Cup are single-masted vessels. They are usually about 24 m (79 ft) in length and weigh 24 tonnes, with most of the weight in the keel – the backbone of the yacht. Designers and builders strive to build a light but strong hull to maximize the yacht's performance.

WORLD races

WORLD races

AMERICA'S CUP	FASTNET RACE	VENDÉE GLOBE	VOLVO OCEAN RACE
The America's Cup is named after the first yacht to win the trophy, the *America*. International teams compete in trials for the right to challenge the cup holder in a race for the trophy.	Held every two years, the Fastnet attracts yachts of all classes and sizes. Off the Atlantic coast of Ireland, competitors sail 978.5 km (608 miles). Yachts sail around the Fastnet Rock.	A single-handed, nonstop yacht race, the Vendée Globe is the ultimate endurance test. Sailors must navigate more than 40,233 km (25,000 miles) around the world.	The Volvo Ocean Race (previously called the Whitbread) takes place every four years. Yacht crews of up to 12 people take on the round-the-world challenge.

Yacht racing

Battling wind, weather, and waves, yacht racing is as much a test of on-board technology as the skills of the sailor. It originated in the 17th century as a pastime for kings, and has developed into a highly organized sport with an established calendar of races and regattas. Yachts are raced in different classes, based on size and tonnage. Many short races take place around buoys or markers close to shorelines, while longer events take place out at sea. Some races involve international teams with large yachts and 20-person crews; others challenge the solo mariner in a test of skill and endurance.

Going solo

The ultimate yachting challenge is the single-handed race. The sailor must battle high winds and choppy seas, all the time positioning or "trimming" the sails to make the most effective use of the wind. They are dependent on on-board satellite navigation equipment to determine their location. In round-the-world races, the solo mariner can go for months without seeing another person.

Teamwork

Team races can involve crews of up to 20 people, each with their own job to do for the duration of the race. Some crew members are responsible for raising and lowering the sails, others for trimming the sails, and some for making tactical decisions. Behind the scenes, yacht designers, builders, engineers, and sailmakers all contribute to competition success.

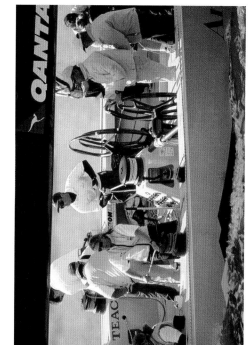

America's CUP

The ultimate prize in the world of yachting is the America's Cup. Since the race began in 1851, the course has covered a range of routes with many nations taking part. The yacht and sail design has developed over time and varies between competing teams, but the roles of the crew stay the same. Each crew member has a set of responsibilities, as well as being on hand to assist other crew mates when necessary. Effective teamwork is integral to winning the cup.

1. **Bowman** Agility is required in this action-packed role. The bowman must handle the triangular spinnaker sail and prepare other sails for raising.

2. **Sail store** The weather conditions and wind speed dictate choice of sail. This is where sails are stored until they are required for use.

3. **Sewerman** The wet, dark sail store is nicknamed the sewer. The sewerman is in charge of packing and organizing the sails, and stays in the store during the race.

4. **Mid-bowman** On deck, the mid-bowman works alongside the bowman, mastman, and pitman to administer sail changes, including to the spinnaker and poles.

5. **Mastman** Together with the pitman, the mastman uses weight and strength to hoist the sails as the grinders take up the slack.

6. **Pitman** Responsible for the front section of the boat, the pitman goes into the pit to help with the ropes around the mast. This role also involves assisting the grinders.

7. **Grinder** When the boat sails towards or away from the wind, huge sudden bursts of strength are required from the grinders to power the winches that trim (set) the sails.

8. **Grinder** Sails are hoisted and trimmed by running ropes around mechanical winches. The grinders power these winches in response to the trimmers' demands.

9. **Trimmer** The trimmers control the spinnaker downwind and the headsail upwind. They help the skipper to decide the best speed.

10. **Trimmer** Experienced trimmers can generate increased speed from their yacht as the situation dictates, even before computers on board can detect it.

11. **Mainsail grinder** The biggest winch on the yacht is the one controlling the mainsail, and manning this is the mainsail grinder's major task.

12. **Traveller** With the assistance of the mainsail trimmer, the traveller trims the mainsail, as well as keeping track of the speed upwind.

13. **Mainsail trimmer** With a sound knowledge of sails and rigging, this type of trimmer controls the ropes that shape the mainsail to generate maximum performance.

14. **Navigator** In charge of the vessel's computers and electronic instruments, the navigator relays weather and route information to the team.

15. **Skipper** The public face of the team, the skipper is responsible for steering the boat, motivating the team, and ultimately, the safety of all on board.

16. **Strategist** The strategist looks out for changes in weather and the wind's speed and direction as these will affect the remainder of the course.

17. **Tactician** As the eyes of the boat, the tactician oversees the boat's tactical position in relation to opposition yachts, wind, and current.

18. **Runner** The rigging that holds tension in the mast must be adjusted every time the boat changes course. The runner controls this with a winch.

All hands on deck

As the America's Cup races are short, there is no accommodation on board for the crew. The deck is crowded with crew, so each person has to stay focused on their individual tasks. The crew must pull together to tackle difficult manoeuvres, high winds, or choppy seas.

Crafting the cup

Inscribed in silver on the ornate America's Cup trophy are the names of all the yachts that have taken part in the race – both winners and challengers. In order to make room for more names, silver bases were introduced and placed under the cup in 1958 and 2001.

Superyacht

New for the 21st century, the 118 WallyPower is the ultimate superyacht. This privately owned, luxury yacht combines the latest engineering with futuristic design. The 36-m (118-ft) motor-powered boat is packed with high-tech systems and luxurious fittings, concealed beneath a sleek, clean exterior. Weighing 95 tonnes and cruising at 110 kph (68 mph), 118 WallyPower has a professional crew and room for six guests to enjoy the high life on the high seas.

Launch boat

A panel in the front deck opens hydraulically to reveal the garage. Inside, a 5.5-m (18-ft) dinghy, known as a tender, is housed. If the guests want to go to shore, a crane launches the tender into the water. When the teak-floor garage is empty, it is used as a gym.

Navigation station

The navigation area resembles a flight deck more than a boat's control centre. This console is used for the start-up, engineering, and monitoring systems. Two other consoles control the steering, communication, and navigation.

Type: Fast motor yacht   **Year built**: 2002   **Shipyard**: Intermarine-Rodriguez, Italy   **Maximum power**: 16,800 HP   **Fuel tank capacity**: 22,000 litres (4,839 gallons)   **Maximum width**: 7.4 m (24 ft)   **Accommodation**: 6 guests, 6 crew

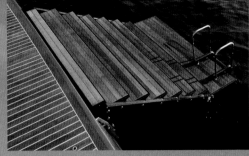

Loft-style lounge
Accessed through an automatic sliding door, the spacious, open lounge area has teak floors, soft cushions, and views through the tinted glass windows. On hot days, when the boat is anchored, this is the coolest part of the vessel.

Diving platform
The two side decks along the superstructure are protected by bulwarks – raised sections above deck. At anchor, these bulwarks drop down hydraulically to increase light, enhance the view, and serve as diving platforms.

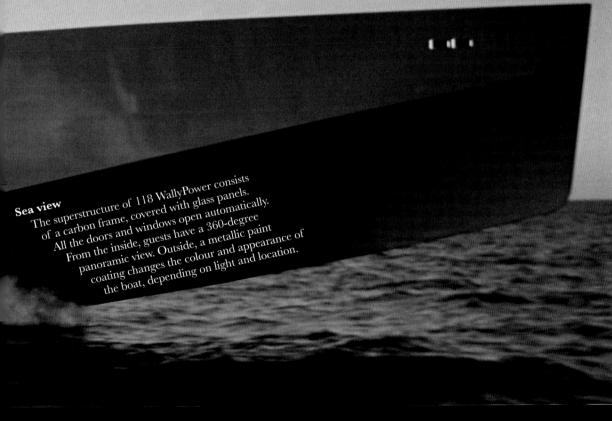

Sea view
The superstructure of 118 WallyPower consists of a carbon frame, covered with glass panels. All the doors and windows open automatically. From the inside, guests have a 360-degree panoramic view. Outside, a metallic paint coating changes the colour and appearance of the boat, depending on light and location.

Superstructure: Carbon fibre and laminated composite glass   **Draught (depth below surface):** 1.36 m (4.5 ft)   **Deck finish:** Teak

Speed tests
The vessel had to undergo extensive testing to ensure its innovative hull design was suited to travelling at top speeds of 130 kph (81 mph). The engines had to be versatile enough to travel at high and low speeds, and in calm and rough seas. Three petrol turbine motors drive the waterjets to achieve the top speed in open water, while two diesel engines power the waterjets for slow sailing in narrow waters.

Profile plan

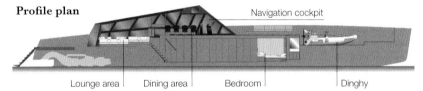

Navigation cockpit

Lounge area   Dining area   Bedroom   Dinghy

Lower layout

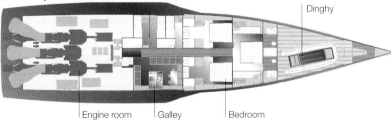

Dinghy

Engine room   Galley   Bedroom

Below deck
The navigation cockpit, diner, and lounge are one continuous, open-plan space. Under the dining area, a skylight illuminates the lower deck. This deck has a vast, sound-proofed engine room where the two diesel engines and three petrol turbines are located. The next compartment is the galley (kitchen), followed by the bedrooms with en suite bathrooms for the guests and the crew.

Cruising

Before air travel became widely available, the ocean liner was the only way to cross oceans and visit other continents. Even today, there is no other way to reach Antarctica. During the early 20th century, liners became famous for the luxury they offered to the highest-paying passengers. There was elegant dining, glittering entertainment, and extravagant balls. Luxury is still one of the main attractions of cruise ships, together with visits to exotic ports en route.

飛鳥II
ASUKA CRUISE
2006.7-2007.7
国内&海外クルーズ

CUNARD LINE
TO ALL PARTS OF THE WORLD

New horizons

In the past, ocean liners were a form of transport for passengers wanting to travel from one destination to another, with luxurious rooms for high-paying first-class passengers and basic cabins for second- and third-class passengers. Although aircraft now have the monopoly on long-distance travel, ocean liners have evolved to become a holiday experience in themselves. Passengers on modern cruise ships enjoy a wide range of on-board facilities, as well as short stops at interesting ports along the way.

On-board dip

Swimming for fun and relaxation became very popular during the 1930s. Cruise liners built in that decade usually had one small indoor pool to satisfy the demand. Today's ships offer a selection of facilities, including indoor and outdoor pools, jacuzzis, saunas, and steam rooms.

Stylish surroundings

Cruise ship interiors have always reflected the fashions and designs of the day. In the 1930s, the dominant look was Art Deco, featuring chrome pillars, lights, mirrors, and gilt. Modern interiors use lightweight, durable materials, and styles are more minimalist with clean, functional lines.

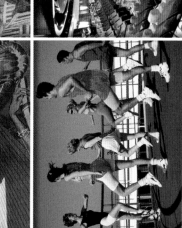

Luxury accommodation

Cabins are graded according to their amenities, with the more expensive accommodation offering sea views or balconies, fresh flowers and fruit, and even butler service. Today, there are extra facilities, including a telephone, television, refrigerator, and en suite bathroom.

Fitness on deck

Many early liners were not equipped with exercise facilities so passsengers used to take a walk around the deck to stretch their legs. There are many more options available today, with passengers participating in regular fitness classes or using state-of-the-art indoor gyms.

Entertainment options

From jazz bands to symphony orchestras, music was the top form of cruise ship entertainment in the past. There were also deck games, such as donkey derbies and a throwing game called quoits. Now ships have cinemas, theatres, casinos, libraries, dance floors, and bingo.

Dining experience

Formal dining characterized the cruise ship experience, with men wearing black tie, women wearing evening gowns, and chefs serving up fine cuisine. Many modern liners offer self-service buffets as well as waiter service. Other informal dining options include cafés, pubs, and poolside bars.

Modern cruises

Several hundred cruise ships are operating around the world today. Their itineraries range from round-the-world trips to mini-breaks around the Mediterranean or Caribbean seas. Other popular destinations include tiny islands in the Pacific Ocean and the scenic Scandinavian fjords.

Queen Mary 2

Luxury liner

Welcome on board the *Queen Mary 2*. Launched in 2004, this enormous cruise liner is the same length as 41 double-decker buses and can carry 2,620 passengers. The vessel spends summers in European waters, while winters are passed across the Atlantic, cruising around the Americas and Canada. The *Queen Mary 2* is expected to sail for 40 years, travelling the equivalent of 12 trips to the Moon.

1 Guests in the Royal Suites dine at the Queen's Grill. The menu changes each evening, but meals can also be made specially to customers' fancy.

2 This is one of five saltwater swimming pools dotted around the ship in various shapes and sizes. Each has a pool bar for drinks and snacks.

3 The nightclub, G32, has a huge dance floor. Rock and hip-hop music is played most nights. During the day, ballroom dancing classes take place.

4 Named after the leading US chef, the Todd English restaurant is a favourite with food critics. Mediterranean cuisine is served inside or alfresco.

5 Past luxury of classic cruise liners is relived in the ornate, three-storey Britannia restaurant, also home to the largest wine cellar at sea.

6 An audio tour, called the Maritime Quest Exhibit, takes passengers back to the golden era of cruising using photographs and wall panels.

7 Children are entertained in the Play Zone. This well-run camp has toys, board games, computer terminals, and a splash pool.

8 In an emergency, there are 14 semi-enclosed lifeboats and eight tender lifeboats, each for 150 people, plus two fast six-person rescue boats.

9 This traditional English pub, The Golden Lion, offers drinks, bar food, karaoke, and televised sports events.

10 The Veuve Clicquot bar serves champagne in fine Waterford flute glasses. A selection of coffees and pastries are available.

11 Roulette wheels, fruit machines, card tables, and dice games are all on show at the exclusive, late-night Empire casino.

12 From evening gowns to sportswear, passengers can enjoy browsing and buying at the Mayfair shopping area.

SUPERSIZE SPECIFICATIONS

The *Queen Mary 2* has 14 decks of sports facilities, bars, shops, cabins, and lounges, as well as 10 restaurants. The height of the vessel is about the same as that of a 23-storey building, while the power room could light a small city. From a distance, the vessel is as easy to hear as it is to spot – the whistle is audible 16 km (10 miles) away!

Cost:	£550 million (US$1 billion)
Length:	345 m (1,132 ft)
Width:	41 m (135 ft)
Height (keel to funnel):	72 m (236 ft)
Speed:	55 kph (34 mph)
Power:	157,000 horsepower engines
Passengers:	2,620
Crew:	1,253

13 In the Grand Lobby, a classical-style staircase, surrounded by cabins on either side, leads down to luxurious seating and modern works of art.

14 The King's Court comprises four restaurants – Asian, Italian, a carvery, and the chef's galley, where guests can watch their meals being prepared.

15 Flowers bloom throughout the year at the colonial-style Winter Garden, while a string quartet adds to the calming ambience.

16 A variety of plays, operas, musicals, readings, and live acts are shown at the Royal Court Theatre. Workshops and drama classes are held for guests.

17 The Canyon Ranch Spa Club is the biggest on any ship. There are 24 treatment rooms, a thermal suite, reflexology basins, and a steam room.

18 The ship has a lecture programme, ConneXions, where topical issues are presented and discussed with experts from leading international institutions.

19 Activities available at the sports centre include a golf driving range, playing field, and a state-of-the-art gym with separate weight room.

20 This floating planetarium is called Illuminations. It also functions as a cinema, 500-seat lecture hall, and broadcasting studio.

21 All the rooms of the Royal Suites have private lift access, whirlpool baths, walk-in wardrobes, en-suite bars, fresh flowers, and 24-hour room service.

22 At the Commodore Club, cocktails are served while live jazz is played against a background panorama of the night sky.

23 This is the world's largest library at sea and guests can learn more about lecture subjects here. A bookshop is located next door.

24 Dotted all around the ship are more than 300 works of art valued at £3 million (US$5.5 million), created by well-known artists.

Switch
The driver presses a button to start the four-second transformation into a marine vehicle. Gibbs Aquada cuts the drive to the wheels, which retract to avoid dragging. The trim tabs (rear plates) adjust to help lift the boat out of the water.

On Land
Gibbs Aquada performs like a sports car, accelerating from 0–96 kph (0–60 mph) in under 10 seconds and travelling at speeds of up to 160 kph (100 mph). However, to prevent water leaks, there are no doors so the driver must climb into the vehicle.

Aquada

Making waves in the world of high-tech, high-performance leisure vehicles is the dual-purpose Gibbs Aquada, equipped to race on roads and cruise in water. At the press of a button, Gibbs Aquada automatically makes the transition from moving on land to working in water. This award-winning vehicle was launched in 2003, after seven years of planning and the efforts of more than 70 engineers and designers. In the future, the vehicle's creators – Gibbs Technologies Ltd – hope to introduce their high-speed water-traversing technology to other types of motor vehicle.

In Water
The same engine that moved Gibbs Aquada on land now provides power to the vehicle's submerged jet. The jet begins expelling water to propel Gibbs Aquada through the water at speeds of 48 kph (30 mph). A water skier can even be towed behind the vehicle!

Interior features

Gibbs Aquada's dashboard displays marine and land speeds, as well as mileage. The seats are made of fully waterproof marine vinyl, and the central seating improves passenger weight distribution on water, especially if the driver is alone. A storage net underneath each seat carries a life jacket.

Technical specifications

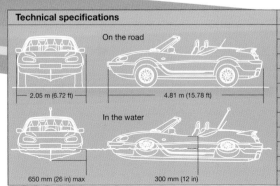

On the road

2.05 m (6.72 ft)   4.81 m (15.78 ft)

In the water

650 mm (26 in) max   300 mm (12 in)

Category	Private Light Vehicle and RCD
Engine	175 hp, 24 valve, V6, 2.5 litre (0.5 gallons)
Gearbox	5-speed auto and reverse
Fuel capacity	67 litres (15 gallons) of 95 Ron Unleaded
Completed	2003
Anti-corrosion	To marine standards
Seating	Three elevated seats
Jet	940 kg (2,072 lb) thrust
Vehicle weight	1,466 kg (3,232 lb)
Buoyancy	Non-sinkable if swamped
Top speeds	Water 48 kph (30 mph), land 160 kph (100 mph)
Lights	Road and marine navigation lights

Aquabatic achievements

■ In 1999, the greatest swim in white water was performed by American Thom Stanton. He swam through 12 km (7 miles) of dangerous, fast-moving rapids.

■ The largest wave successfully surfed was 21.3 m (70 ft) in height. It was ridden in 2004 by American Pete Cabrinha at a place known as "Jaws" (Peahi) on Maui in Hawaii.

■ In 2005, American George Blair became the oldest water-skier when he water-skied across Lake Florence in Florida aged 90.

■ American kite surfers Fabrice Collard, Kent Marincovik, and Neil Hutchinson made the longest continuous kite-surfing journey when they travelled 163 km (101 miles) from Key West to Cuba in 1991.

■ In 2000, Englishman Shaun Baker made the fastest-ever canoe descent when he descended a vertical height of 22.8 m (75 ft) in 19.9 seconds on a river in Wales.

■ The record for most people riding a wave on a surfboard at one time was achieved by a 14-strong team in Cornwall, England, on 22 July 2003. The giant surfboard measured a staggering 11 m (37 ft).

Surfing

The first recorded document to describe surfing dates back to the 18th century. After the death of explorer Captain Cook in 1779, Lieutenant James King completed Cook's journals and included observations of surfing with a narrow board. Competitive surfing is very popular, but searching for the biggest waves, known as "rhino hunting", is also a favourite pursuit. When a surfer is knocked over by a wave, it is called a "wipeout".

Aquabatics

Watersports have been gaining popularity since the 1950s, when surfing first took off and the mass production of pleasure boats began. A combination of classic watersports and imaginative new craft means the oceans are alive with adventure and activity, as people find ever more exciting ways to ride the waves.

Windsurfing

This wind-powered sport began in the 1960s in the USA and became an Olympic event in 1984. By the 1990s, its popularity waned as the equipment became too specialized and complicated to use. Recently, the development of basic board and sail designs, aimed at beginners, has renewed interest in windsurfing.

Kayaking

The Inuit, an Arctic people, developed the kayak, meaning "man's boat". It is similar to a canoe, but single-paddled and sealed, so, if the kayak overturns, water will not leak inside. The first kayaks were made of wood covered in sealskin. Fibreglass, carbon, and plastic are used today.

Jet skiing

First invented in the 1970s, these engine-propelled craft use jets to expel water and can travel at speeds of 60 kph (37 mph). Modern jet skis are equipped with a lanyard – a switch to cut the engine if the rider falls. Jet skis are gaining in popularity as they are relatively cheap to buy and give the owner freedom to ride the seas.

Dragon boat racing

About 2,500 years ago, dragon boat racing began in southern China and has since spread across the world. The boats are decorated with dragon heads at the bow and tails at the stern. The standard crew of 22 consists of 10 pairs of paddlers, a steerer, and a drummer, whose beating dictates the timing of the paddle strokes.

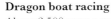

Kite surfing

This sport developed from surfing. A surfer, attached to a board, manoeuvres a kite in the wind and gets carried along. In strong winds on calm water, a kite-surfer can travel at speeds of 50 kph (31 mph). "Airtime" refers to how long a kite-surfer is lifted clean out of the water. The record stands at 8.9 seconds!

White water rafting

Turbulent river waves are known as white water. A six-tier classification system exists to inform rafters of the difficulty of each river. Class one means easy to navigate, but class six carries the risk of death! Manageable rapids in South America and Canada are the most popular.

River boats

Over the centuries, all kinds of vessels have been built for travelling along inland waterways. River boats may have to contend with sand banks or hidden rocks, so they often have a shallow hull. The exact design depends on local materials and how the boat will be used, for example short fishing trips or transporting heavy goods. Some river boats are complete mobile homes, with a galley (kitchen) and berths for sleeping in.

Plank boats
In the state of Kerala, in southwestern India, people make huge boats called kettuvalams. Some are 25 m (82 ft) long. Constructed from wooden planks, each tied to the next with coir (coconut) rope, the boats were traditionally used to transport rice, coconuts, and spices. Today, many have been converted into houseboats for tourists.

Floating markets
Early in the mornings, Thailand's floating markets open for trade on rivers and canals. Sellers arrive in boats laden with vegetables, flowers, and fruits. The boats stay near the water's edge, so customers on land can view the goods. The largest floating market is in Ratchaburi, 80 km (50 miles) southwest of Bangkok.

City of gondolas

The Italian city of Venice is built on a series of islands linked by 150 canals. There are no roads for cars, so the only way to travel is on foot or by boat. Venice is known for its long, narrow gondolas, rowed by gondoliers, but ordinary Venetians usually travel by *vaporetto* (water bus).

High-altitude homes

Lying more than 3,800 m (12,467 ft) above sea level, Lake Titicaca in the Andes mountains is the world's highest navigable (deep enough for boats) lake. The Uros Indians live there on islands built from a reed called totora. Their boats are made from the same material. The Uros use the boats to hunt ducks, fish in the lake, and visit islands nearby.

Full steam ahead

The Mississippi River, which flows through the southern USA, is famous for its paddle steamers. They are powered by a steam engine, which drives a paddle wheel. As the wheel turns, the paddles push through the water and the boat moves forwards. Some steamers are floating museums or casinos, but most carry tourists on trips.

Busy with barges

Amsterdam, in the Netherlands, has about 2,500 houseboats along its numerous canals. Many boats are former Dutch barges, which were originally built to carry freight and have since been converted into homes. Along the city's Singel Canal, a regular flower market is held on the barges.

Bridges

Spanning rivers and canals, bridges provide a passage for people to cross. Although many bridges are fixed structures, sometimes they must be moveable to allow people to pass over and boats to go underneath. Depending on the design, a bridge may lift, swing, tilt, fold, curl up, or even sink!

Going up

The Falkirk Wheel in central Scotland connects two canals that have a height difference of 35 m (115 ft). In the past, barges had to pass through 11 locks to get between levels, but now the rotating wheel lifts them instead.

Going down

Instead of raising its deck to allow boats through, a submersible bridge lowers into the water. There is a submersible bridge at either end of the Corinth Canal in Greece. To let boats pass, each one sinks to the bottom of the 8-m- (26-ft-) deep canal.

The upper gondola carries barges to the Forth and Clyde Canal.

Aqueduct support

The gondola holds four 20-m (66-ft) barges. Cogs keep it level at all times.

The arm turns on a central cog attached to the aqueduct support.

Hanging platform

Known as a transporter bridge, this structure crosses the River Nervión in Spain. A gondola (platform) for cars hangs on long wires from its extremely high span. This gondola is moved across the river by traction when no ships are passing under. Only about 20 transporter bridges were ever built, and just eight are still in use.

Reinforced concrete aqueduct (water channel) leads to the Union Canal.

Gondola is held by wires, fixed to wheels on tracks, that span the bridge.

Folding bridge

The Hörnbrücke is a folding footbridge in Kiel, northern Germany. It was built in 1997 to take passengers from the city centre to the ferry port. Every hour, the Hörnbrücke folds into the shape of the letter "N" so large vessels can pass through and up the River Hörn.

Tilting bridge

Built to carry foot traffic and cyclists, the Gateshead Millennium Bridge spans the River Tyne in northeast England. Two hydraulic pumps provide the power to tilt the bridge. As the top arch tilts lower, the pathway rises and makes room for boats underneath.

One-minute wonder

Completed in 1893, London's Tower Bridge can be raised in just one minute to allow tall ships to pass under it. The bridge still uses the original hydraulic system to lift the bridge halves, or bascules. The bridge is raised about 900 times every year.

Smallest submarine

In 1991, English engineer William Smith built the world's tiniest submarine, *Water Beatle*. At just 2.95 m (9 ft 6 in) long, 1.15 m (3 ft 7 in) wide, and 1.42 m (4 ft 6 in) high, *Water Beatle* is smaller than a Mini car. It has three air cylinders, allowing it to stay underwater for more than four hours.

Biggest boat tie-up

At the 2003 Raft-Off Regatta on Lake Norman in the USA, 944 boats were tied together in a continual free-floating line.

Largest hovercraft

The British SRN4 MK II hovercraft is 56 m (184 ft) in length and weighs 310 tonnes. On board, there is room for 418 passengers and 60 cars. The hovercraft's top speed is 120 kph (75 mph).

Longest pedal-boat journey

Between October 1992 and February 1993, Japanese record-breaker Kenichi Horie travelled from Hawaii in the USA to Okinawa in Japan by pedal boat. It took him almost four months to cover the distance of 7,500 km (4,660 miles).

Largest propeller

Japanese Shipbuilders Stone Manganese Marine Ltd designed and manufactured a giant six-bladed propeller. It has a width of 9 m (29.5 ft) and weighs a hefty 93.5 tonnes.

Longest canal

China's Grand Canal connects Hang Zhou in the south to Beijing in the north. First constructed by manual labourers in 283 CE, it was rebuilt between 1958–72 to a length of 1,795 km (1,115 miles).

Fastest propeller-driven boat

In 2004, off the California coast in the USA, American David Villwock achieved a record-breaking speed of 355 kph (220 mph) in a hydroplane.

Greatest car-carrier

The ferry *Ulysses*, belonging to Irish Ferries, was launched in 2000. Not only is there room for 1,342 cars, but it can also carry a staggering 59,925 passengers, too.

Water records

The challenge of choppy seas, strong currents, and severe gales is not enough for some sailors and watersports enthusiasts. Instead, they are busy making a huge splash in the record books by such feats as constructing the world's biggest sail, largest yacht, and smallest submarine, as well as pedalling a tiny boat across a vast ocean.

Most valuable shipwreck
In 1985, the wreck of Spanish ship *Nuestra Senora de Atocha* was discovered off the coast of Florida in the USA. It sank in 1622, taking with it a haul of gold and silver weighing 40 tonnes, as well as 32 kg (70 lb) of emeralds.

Biggest sail
US sailmakers Doyle created a single sail with an area of 1,833 sq m (19,730 sq ft). This enormous sail was attached to the mast of the superyacht *Mirabella V* in 2002.

Longest canoe
Built in 1940 in New Zealand, the Maori war canoe *Nga Toki Matawhaorua* is 36 m (118 ft) in length and 2 m (6ft 6 in) wide. The canoe is big enough to carry 135 people.

Water speed record
Every year, challengers attempt to beat the record for the official fastest speed of any waterborne vehicle. It still stands with Australian Ken Warby. In 1978, Warby took his vehicle *Spirit of Australia* to a top speed of 510 kph (317 mph).

Wave-rider
In April 2006, British surfer Steve King rode a continuous wave for 12 km (7.5 miles) along the Severn Estuary. He stayed upright for 77 minutes in total.

Biggest steamboat
The New Orleans steamboat *American Queen* is 127 m (417 ft) long, the same length as 11 double-decker buses. The luxurious steamboat weighs 4,891 tonnes, has six ...ks, and capacity for 450 passengers.

Largest yacht
The Saudi Arabian royal yacht *Abdul Aziz* is an incredible 147 m (482 ft) long – the same length as 21 killer whales lined up one after the other! Built in Denmark and furnished in England, *Abdul Aziz* is worth more than £57 million (US$104 million).

Deepest diving submersible in service
The Japanese submersible *Shinkai 6500* carries three people and is used for deep-sea research. It can dive to depths of 6,500 m (21,325 ft), as its name suggests.

Land

Timeline

MODEL OF EARLY WHEEL

The wheel
The first wheel is made from three planks pegged together and cut into a circle. These heavy, solid wheels are fitted onto axles with pegs and are used to carry the first carts.

EARLY PUBLIC BUS

Public bus
The first horse-drawn public bus is introduced in Paris, France, by inventor Blaise Pascal. The bus service has a regular route, timetable, and fare system.

LONDON UNDERGROUND SIGN

Underground rail
The world's first underground rail service is introduced in London. The noisy, steam-powered railway runs for 6 km (3.7 miles) across the city.

EARLY DUTCH TRAM

Electric trams
The first electric tram is built by German engineer Werner von Siemens in Berlin. Cities around the world replace their horse-hauled tramways with electric systems.

GRUNER TAXIMETER

Fairer fares
German Wilhelm Bruhn invents the modern taximeter. The device is used to measure the time and distance a taxi travels. This information enables cab drivers to accurately charge their customers.

c. 3500 BCE · c. 2000 BCE · 1662 · 1804 · 1863 · 1871 · 1881 · 1885 · 1891 · 1908

War chariots
Horse-drawn chariots provide ancient civilizations, such as the Egyptians, Greeks, and Mesopotamians, with speedy vehicles to use in battles held on flat, open ground.

MODEL OF A CHARIOT

Steam locomotion
British engineer Richard Trevithick builds the first steam-powered railway locomotive. The four-wheeled engine travels at a top speed of 8 kph (5 mph) and can haul wagons weighing 10 tonnes.

MODEL OF TREVITHICK'S STEAM ENGINE

PENNY FARTHING

Cycling craze
The Penny Farthing is invented and becomes a popular bicycle. The large front wheel measures around 1.5 m (59 in) in diameter, and enables riders to cross greater distances, while pedalling less.

Motorcycle
German inventor Gottlieb Daimler attaches a petroleum-powered four-stroke engine to a wooden bicycle and creates the world's first motorcycle.

DAIMLER'S MOTORCYCLE

Ford's Model T
Henry Ford builds the Model T in Detroit, USA. Ford soon introduces a moving assembly line, dramatically cutting down labour costs. The Model T is widely considered to be the first affordable car.

HENRY FORD'S MODEL T

Red to green

The first red-green automated electric traffic lights are developed by Lester Wire, a policeman from Salt Lake City, USA. Amber lights and buzzers are added later.

EARLY TRAFFIC LIGHTS

NAPIER-CAMPBELL'S BLUEBIRD

Land-speed record

Sir Malcolm Campbell's Napier-Campbell Bluebird is the first vehicle purpose-built to break the land-speed record, driving a record-breaking 281.44 kph (174.88 mph).

Skateboarding

Wooden skateboards are commercially produced for the first time in California, USA. A skateboarding craze spreads across the USA and to other parts of the world.

EARLY WOODEN SKATEBOARD

BMX STUNT RIDER

Stunt bike

BMX (bicycle motocross) emerges in California, USA. With small, 50.8-cm (20-in) knobby tyres, BMX bikes are originally built to race on sandy, hilly tracks. BMX freestyle, where riders perform tricks, develops from BMX racing.

THRUSTSSC

Sound barrier

British RAF pilot, Andy Green, drives the ThrustSSC to set a new land-speed record of 1,227.99 kph (763.035 mph) in the Black Rock Desert, USA. The ThrustSSC is also the first land vehicle to break the sound barrier at Mach 1.

▲1912 ▲1927 ▲1960s ▲1970s ▲1997
1916▼ 1958▼ 1964▼ 1994▼ 2004▼

Armoured tank

The army tank is invented by the British for use in World War I. The tank's heavy riveted metal armour protects the soldiers inside from weapon fire, and the unique flat "caterpillar tracks" can traverse muddy, uneven terrain.

BRITISH MARK V TANK

Super seller

The Honda Super Cub is introduced and goes on to become the world's best-selling motor vehicle, with sales exceeding 35 million bikes.

HONDA SUPER CUB

Bullet train

The world's first high-speed rail service begins with Japan's *Shinkansen* (bullet train). The first bullet train travels 535 km (332 miles) between Tokyo and Osaka in under four hours, reaching speeds of 200 kph (124 mph).

JAPANESE BULLET TRAIN

Tunnel link

The Channel Tunnel between Britain and mainland Europe is completed, stretching 50 km (31 miles) and lying 40 m (131 ft) beneath the English Channel. It consists of three tunnels: two are for trains, while a third tunnel is for maintenance workers and emergency access.

CHANNEL TUNNEL TERMINAL

Hybrid car

The Toyota Prius is the world's first mass-produced, mid-sized hybrid car. The car switches between a petrol-powered engine and an emission-free electric motor.

TOYOTA PRIUS

Traffic controls

Stop! Go! Give way! One way! Wrong way! Around the world, signs and signals enforce traffic rules, and safely direct motor vehicles, cyclists, and pedestrians on the roads. The simple words, bright colours, and bold graphic symbols ensure that road users quickly understand what the traffic instruction means.

Pedestrian crossing (the Netherlands)
This is called a "zebra crossing" in the USA and UK because of the stripes.

BUS ZONE
3.00 PM – 6.30 PM
MON-FRI →

NO STOPPING

LOADING ZONE
7.00 AM – 3.00 PM
MON-FRI

30

No parking zones (Australia)
This area is restricted to buses and vehicles loading goods.

Speed limit (France)
The speed limit on many urban roads is 30 kph (18.6 mph).

Bike lane (Austria)
Only bicycles can travel in this designated lane.

DETOUR

INTERSTATE 295 **INTERSTATE 395**

SOUTH

Signpost (USA)
Signposts can be crammed with traffic information.

7 ST NW 100

No entry (France)
Traffic is not allowed to proceed any further.

Double lines (UK)
Yellow double lines indicate "no parking" zones.

UACHTARÁRD TOUGHTERARD 7½
GAILLIMH GALWAY 2

Directions post (Ireland)
Road users are given the distances to towns

Melting snow (Canada)
Heavy snow melting from rooftops can be dangerous to passers-by.

Stop sign (Morocco)
Red octagons signal "stop" in many parts of the world.

Wild elk (Canada)
Animals such as wild elk can be a hazard on forest roads.

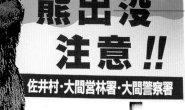

ATTENTION!

熊 出 没
注 意 !!
佐井村・大間営林署・大間警察署

Wild bears (Japan)
Forest visitors are warned that bears are in the vicinity.

قف

7-9:30AM 4-6:30PM MONDAY-FRIDAY

L 100 SCRIOB SCREEBE 5

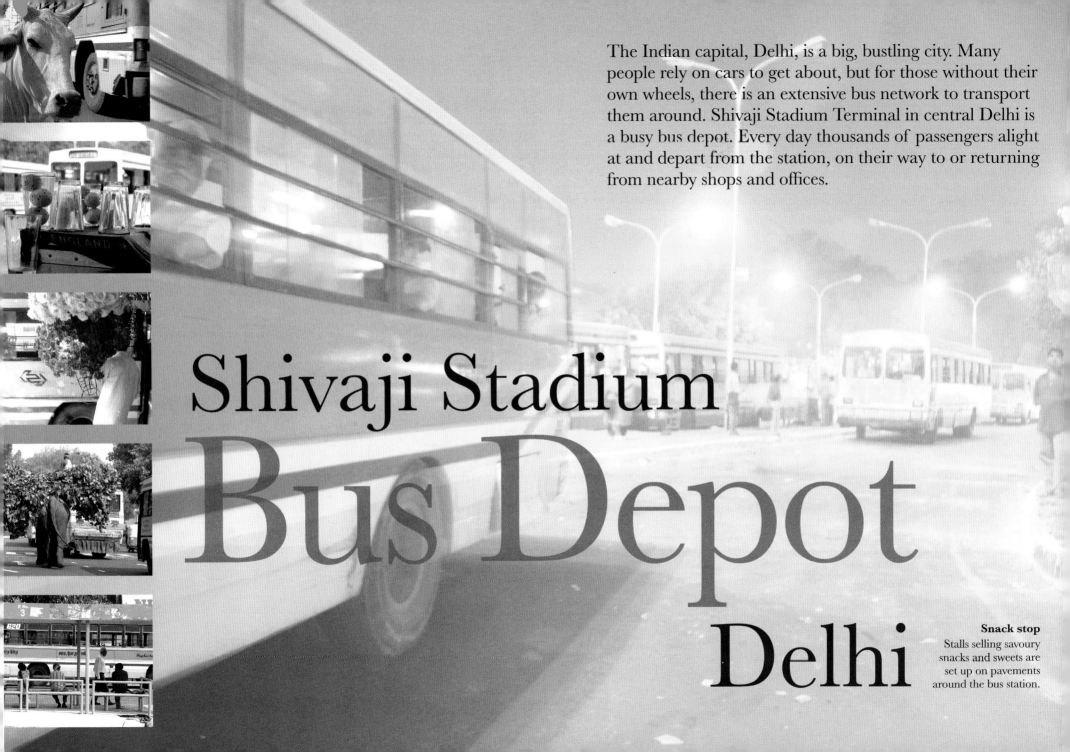

The Indian capital, Delhi, is a big, bustling city. Many people rely on cars to get about, but for those without their own wheels, there is an extensive bus network to transport them around. Shivaji Stadium Terminal in central Delhi is a busy bus depot. Every day thousands of passengers alight at and depart from the station, on their way to or returning from nearby shops and offices.

Shivaji Stadium
Bus Depot
Delhi

Snack stop
Stalls selling savoury snacks and sweets are set up on pavements around the bus station.

The passengers

For the passengers arriving and departing from Shivaji Stadium Terminal every day, buses are a cheap and convenient way of getting around the city. Some use the buses to commute to work or school, while others use them to go shopping or visit friends.

Vikas and Aakash

Brothers Vikas and Aakash make the hour-long journey to school by bus. "We enjoy the ride with our friends."

Raju

Vendor Raju sells plastic toy balls at the station. He carries his stock to and from home every day on a bus. "I have to pay an extra fare for my stock," he explains.

Pallavi

Relaxing after a shopping trip, Pallavi stops for a snack before catching a bus home. "I like riding the bus," she says. "I find them hassle-free."

Anil

Sculptor Anil is on his way to view some exhibitions. "I am a keen observer of people, and the buses in Delhi carry lots of good subjects for me."

Roshni

"The bus is cheaper than a taxi or auto-rickshaw," says Roshni, who is travelling to a hospital across the city for a check-up.

Sudhir

A regular bus user, Sudhir travels 15 km (9 miles) every day to a market near the terminal to buy flowers. "I carry them back on the bus to sell in my shop."

On board

"Munchie" vendors board buses at the depot and at busy stops to sell fruit and snacks to the passengers. Buses can get very crowded, especially during rush hours, when some passengers have to stand and hold on to an overhead bar.

Getting around

- Delhi is one of India's largest cities with a population of 13.8 million people.
- Buses are the most popular form of public transport in the city.
- 1.98 million passengers travel on buses in Delhi every day and 72.6 million bus journeys are made every year.
- A Green Card – a day pass for all Delhi buses – costs 25 rupees (32p).
- The bus system is often referred to by locals as "Daudo to Chado" ("Run to Climb") because of the very short stoppage times at bus stops.
- There are 24,774 buses on the roads of Delhi, compared to 1.3 million cars, 2.7 million motorcycles and scooters, 74,906 auto-rickshaws, and 14,941 taxis.
- Inter-State bus services connect Delhi with other parts of North India, and a bus service operates between Delhi and Lahore, Pakistan.

73

Traffic lights (India)
Traffic lights glow red, amber, and green to tell vehicles whether to stop, wait, or go.

Autorickshaw stand (India)
People can queue for an autorickshaw at this stand.

No right turn

Street sign (Israel)
The name of this street is written in Hebrew, Arabic, and Latin.

וַיָּה דוֹלוֹרוֹזָה
طريق الآلام
VIA DOLOROSA

Traffic control centre (UK)
Masses of closed-circuit television (CCTV) screens in traffic control centres show engineers the status of traffic on the roads. With this information, engineers can detect accidents and monitor congestion.

No horns (Egypt)
Noise pollution can be a problem in big cities. This sign forbids the use of car horns.

SALACH ESS 9½
HÁN DEN 23 T71
OICHEAD MHAMA 5 L
AAM BRIDGE 100
ONÁN EENANE 13

Δράμα Drama 36
Θεσσαλονίκη Thesaloniki 161

Directions sign (Greece)
Highway users are informed of the distances to towns they are approaching.

Customs sign (Croatia)
A customs checkpoint is located at the border.

CARINA
DOUANE

鷹峯 Takagamine 宝ヶ池 Takaragaike
鞍馬 Kurama 修学院 Shugakuin
40 北山通り 103
国立京都国際会館 → Kyoto International Conference Hall 2.5Km

Directions sign (Japan)
Directions are given to nearby towns, tourist attractions, and motorways.

The workers

Drivers, conductors, mechanics, and traffic inspectors work together to ensure the bus services run efficiently and on time. The state-run Delhi Transport Corporation (DTC) is the largest of the city's bus companies.

Sahab
"I get to talk to a lot of people on my route, so time passes really quickly," explains bus conductor Sahab.

Hansraj
"I make the garlands myself," says Hansraj. He sells flower garlands to bus drivers who put them on Hindu shrines in the front of their buses.

Inderjeet
Traffic inspector Inderjeet has been working for the DTC for 38 years. "When I started, the Shivaji hockey stadium hadn't even been built!"

S A Khan
"I start my shift at 6 am and finish at 2.30 pm," says time keeper S A Kahn. He checks that buses arrive and depart from the terminal on schedule.

Karamveer
"I get paid on a kilometre basis, so the more I work and the more I drive, the more I earn," says DTC bus driver Karamveer.

On the road
It is not just other vehicles that Delhi's bus drivers must look out for. Elephants and camels are sometimes ridden along the roads by their owners. Cows, which are sacred to the Hindu religion, can also roam the streets.

Bus business

■ The Delhi Transport Corporation (DTC) runs 3,200 buses from its own fleet and about 2,600 buses from private contractors.
■ The DTC network of buses has a total of 300 routes across the city.

■ Around 29,200 people are employed by the DTC, including drivers, conductors, traffic supervisors, repair and maintenance and administrative staff.
■ All buses, taxis, and auto-rickshaws must

have CNG (compressed natural gas) engines to help combat pollution in the city.
■ Buses, taxis, and auto-rickshaws older than 15 years are banned in Delhi.
■ A metro rail system is being constructed

in the city to help combat the chronic road congestion. The first underground lines opened in 2005.
■ The DTC operates bus routes to connect commuters with the new metro stations.

■ 67 per cent of urban roads are congested during rush hour.

■ The phrase "rush hour" was first used in 1898.

■ The UK is Europe's most-congested country, with 10,000 jams a week.

■ In 1960, 4 per cent of the world's population owned a car.

■ Today, 12 per cent of the world's population own a car.

■ The time lost to traffic jams in a large city is the equivalent to seven people's entire working lives every day.

■ In the USA, people spend more than 100 hours a year commuting.

■ New York City's traffic crawls at an average 10 kph (6.2 mph).

■ The M25 around London is the busiest road in Europe.

■ Drivers in Seattle, USA, are stuck in jams for about 60 hours a year.

■ Weekday traffic speeds in Shanghai, China, are just 9 kph (5.5 mph).

■ In 45 BCE, Rome banned all vehicles from the city because of traffic jams.

■ Almost 13 million cars were recycled in 1997 – this would create a line of traffic circling Earth one and a quarter times.

■ The European Union organizes an annual car-free day so that people can experience jam-free cities.

■ The longest traffic jam ever was 176 km (109 miles) long, stretching from Lyon to Paris, France, on 16 February 1980.

■ The highest traffic jam was at a pass in the Dangla Mountains in China, where more than 1,000 vehicles queued in 2004.

■ Signals from mobile phones are used to work out traffic jam hotspots in Finland.

Traffic jam

Have you ever been on a motorway when the traffic starts to slow down? Bumper to bumper, a queue of cars crawls along ahead of you. You're in a jam! There are more than 500 million motor vehicles in the world today, and, if present trends continue, the number of cars on Earth will double within 30 years; by which time, scientists predict, traffic congestion will become 10 times worse than it is today.

■ Jams cost a typical city £495 million (US$900 million) in lost work time every year.

■ The average commuter spends 46 hours in jams.

■ In 1868, the first traffic lights controlled horse-drawn carriages and pedestrians in London.

■ In Athens, Greece, only cars with odd-numbered licence plates can drive in the city on odd-numbered days, and vice versa for even-numbered cars.

■ On 12 April 1990, a record jam of 18 million cars was reported on the East-West German border as Soviet rule came to an end.

■ A hospital in Norway had to build a new road lane as people kissing loved ones goodbye were causing traffic jams.

■ Traffic police in parts of Asia wear face masks to protect themselves from traffic fumes.

■ In India, cows are a major cause of traffic jams. Considered sacred, they are free to wander onto roads.

■ UN-trained traffic police have controlled the daily jams in Monrovia, Liberia, since the city's traffic lights stopped working in 1990.

■ The longest traffic jam in Japanese history was 135 km (84 miles) long and involved 15,000 vehicles.

■ Traffic jams use up to 26 billion litres (5.7 billion gallons) of fuel each year. The world's oil reserves could run out in less than 100 years.

Car construction

The Gläserne Manufaktur ("transparent factory") in Dresden, Germany, handles the final assembly of the Volkswagen Phaeton car. The factory was specially designed to make car construction visible to visitors and people living nearby. It has walls made entirely of glass and oval-shaped floors with embedded conveyor belts. Most of the work is carried out by hand, by highly skilled factory workers. Robots are only used to transport parts around the factory and undertake heavy, arduous tasks. Customers can visit the factory and get involved in every stage of the construction of their own custom-made car, from selecting the colour and the interior finish, to watching the parts being fitted.

1 Preassembled components are delivered to a warehouse on the outskirts of the city. They are taken as needed to the factory on a specially developed tram, the "CarGoTram".

2 Parts for each car are stacked onto trolleys. It takes eight trolley-loads to make each car. Once loaded, the trolleys are taken by robot to the factory floor.

3 A car's suspension and drivetrain (all the parts that power the car, including the engine) are worked on separately from the body of the car.

4 A slow-moving conveyor belt built into the floor carries the car bodies around the factory. Workers are responsible for different tasks, such as wiring lights and fitting seats.

5 The drivetrain is connected with the car body in a process called the "marriage". The entire procedure, including bolt-fastening, is automated.

6 Robots are used for any heavy work. One robot fits the storage for the spare wheel, another fits the wheels on the car, and a third fits the front and rear windscreens.

7 When constuction is finished, the car is thoroughly checked and tested. Visual checks of the paint finish and body panels are conducted in large light booths.

4

5

7

Delivery time
After their sales documents are processed, customers can look at the information boards to check on the progress of their car delivery and find out which bay they need to go to for collection.

Tower storage
Cars to be delivered that day are brought on an automated conveyor belt from the factory to the car tower. A central lift carries the cars up the tower to a bay allocated by the tower's computer system.

Car lift
The computer system is programmed with a schedule of the day's car deliveries. It instructs one of the two lifts to rise up to the correct bay in the tower. A robotic arm slides out from the lift and reaches under the car, raising it slightly so it can be conveyed onto the lift. Once loaded, the lift descends to the drive-out level.

Car tower

Instead of collecting their new vehicles from a car dealer, Volkswagen customers in Europe can travel to the Autostadt, an automobile-inspired theme park in Wolfsburg, Germany. While car owners wander around the pavilions, their brand-new cars travel by conveyor belt from the nearby factory to be stored in two fully automated 48-m- (160-ft-) high glass towers. When it is time for a car to be delivered to its new owner, a huge mechanical lift swings into action, locates the bay the car is held in, and lowers it to the ground, where another conveyor belt takes it to the delivery bay.

AUTOTÜRME
The cylindrical AutoTürme (car tower) combines the technologies of three classic inventions – the multistorey car park, the forklift truck, and the lift – to create a unique high-rise stacking system. A central mechanism in the tower operates two lifts, which convey vehicles to and from the 400 car bays.

Specifications:	
Height	48 m (158 ft)
Number of storeys	20
Number of car bays	400
Despatch frequency	Every 45 seconds
Lift speed	7 kph (4.5 mph)
Lift rotation	270 degrees
Time it takes to reach distribution centre from tower	4 minutes

Belt to bay

From the tower, the cars are taken on robotic pallets along a conveyor belt to one of four bays. When the car arrives in a bay, the doors open and a member of staff drives the car to the fine finish area.

Fine finish

The final checks of the car take place in the fine finish area. There can be as many as 280 different points to check, including the paintwork and interior finish. The number plate is fitted and the car is ready.

Customer collection

The customer is handed the keys of the car and can drive away.

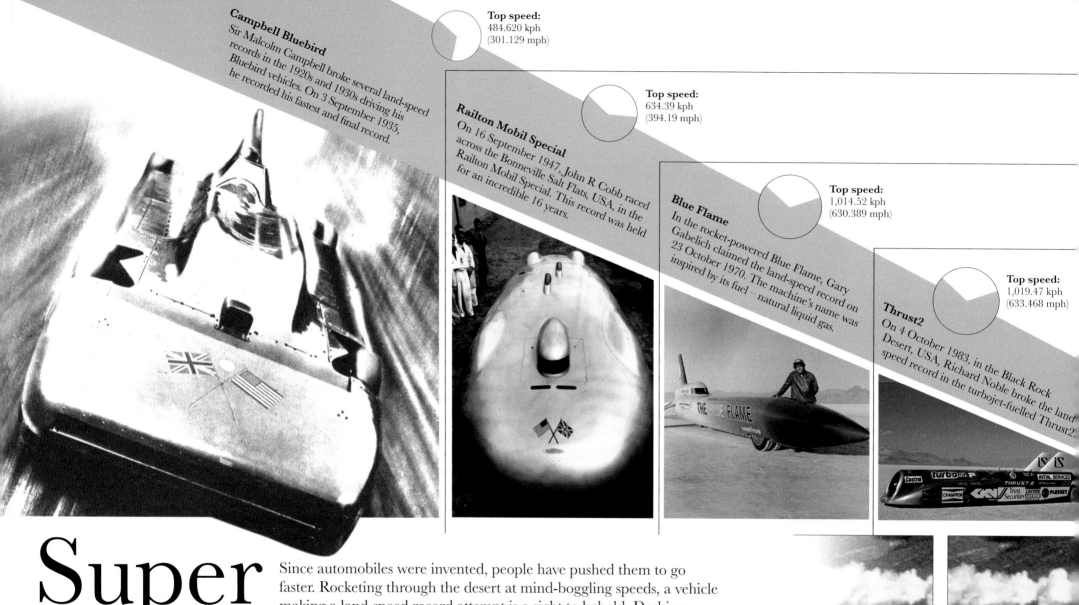

Campbell Bluebird
Sir Malcolm Campbell broke several land-speed records in the 1920s and 1930s driving his Bluebird vehicles. On 3 September 1935, he recorded his fastest and final record.

Top speed:
484.620 kph
(301.129 mph)

Railton Mobil Special
On 16 September 1947, John R Cobb raced across the Bonneville Salt Flats, USA, in the Railton Mobil Special. This record was held for an incredible 16 years.

Top speed:
634.39 kph
(394.19 mph)

Blue Flame
In the rocket-powered Blue Flame, Gary Gabelich claimed the land-speed record on 23 October 1970. The machine's name was inspired by its fuel – natural liquid gas.

Top speed:
1,014.52 kph
(630.389 mph)

Thrust2
On 4 October 1983, in the Black Rock Desert, USA, Richard Noble broke the land speed record in the turbojet-fuelled Thrust2.

Top speed:
1,019.47 kph
(633.468 mph)

Super speed

Since automobiles were invented, people have pushed them to go faster. Rocketing through the desert at mind-boggling speeds, a vehicle making a land-speed record attempt is a sight to behold. Dashing into the record books, land-speed record drivers risk life and limb on their brief and volatile journeys. Fired with jet or rocket-engine thrust, land-speed record vehicles look more like spaceships dreamed up in science fiction films than cars.

Record breakers!

- The world's first land-speed record was made in 1898 by Parisian Count Gaston de Chasseloup-Laubat. Driving 1 km (0.62 miles) in 57 seconds, his car's top speed was 63.13 kph (39.24 mph).
- In 1904, the 160.93-kph (100-mph) land-speed record was broken by Louis Emile Rigolly of France. After losing a race to a fierce rival, he drove his car as fast as he could, reaching 166.64 kph (103.55 mph).
- In 1927, Sir Malcolm Campbell's Napier-Campbell Bluebird was the first vehicle purpose-built to break the land-speed record.
- In 1970, Gary Gabelich's Blue Flame was the first to succeed in breaking the 1,000 kph (621.37 mph) land-speed record.
- The Budweiser Rocket Car is claimed to have broken the sound barrier in 1979. However, the record wasn't counted as it didn't meet international regulations.

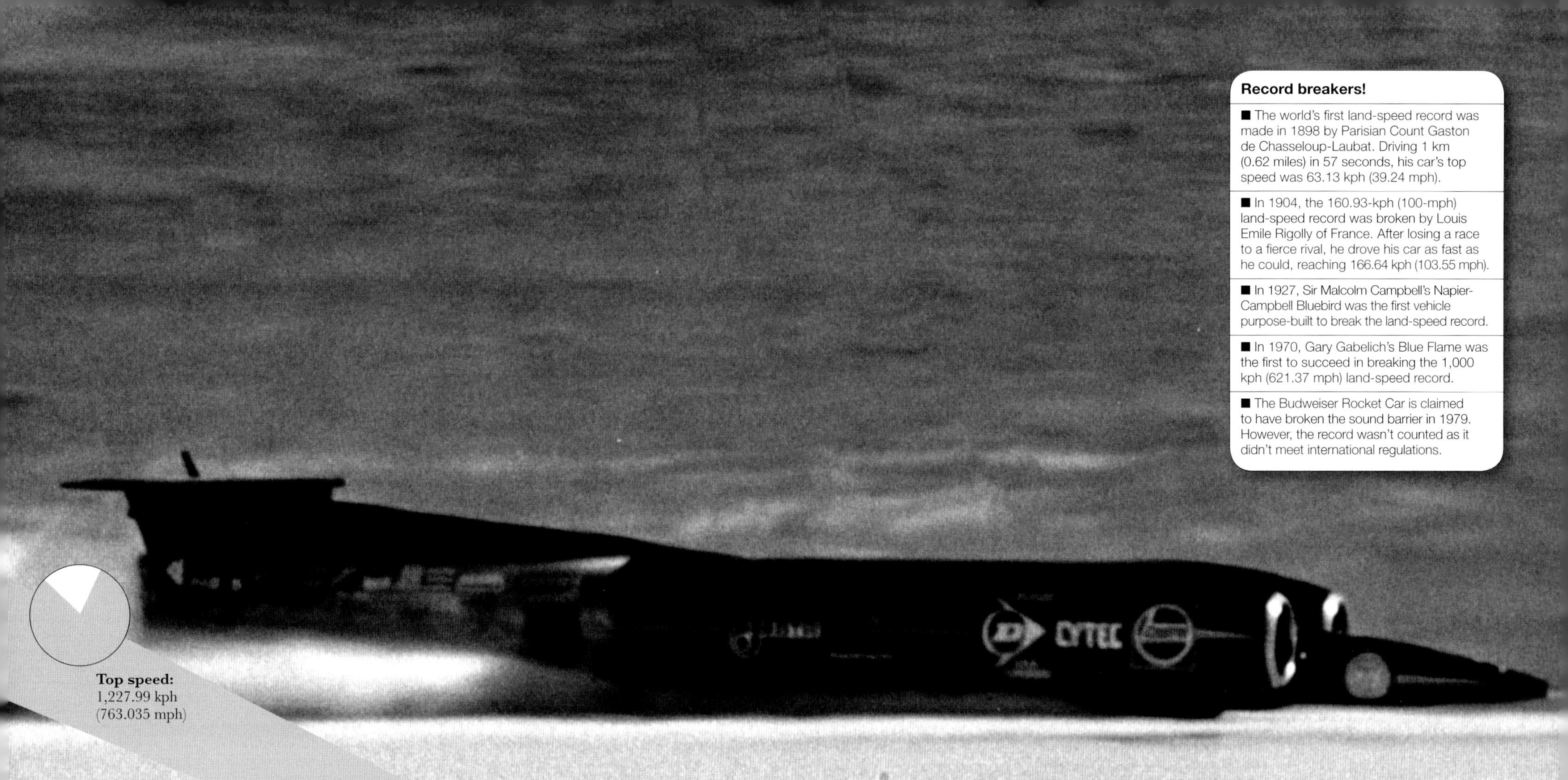

Top speed:
1,227.99 kph
(763.035 mph)

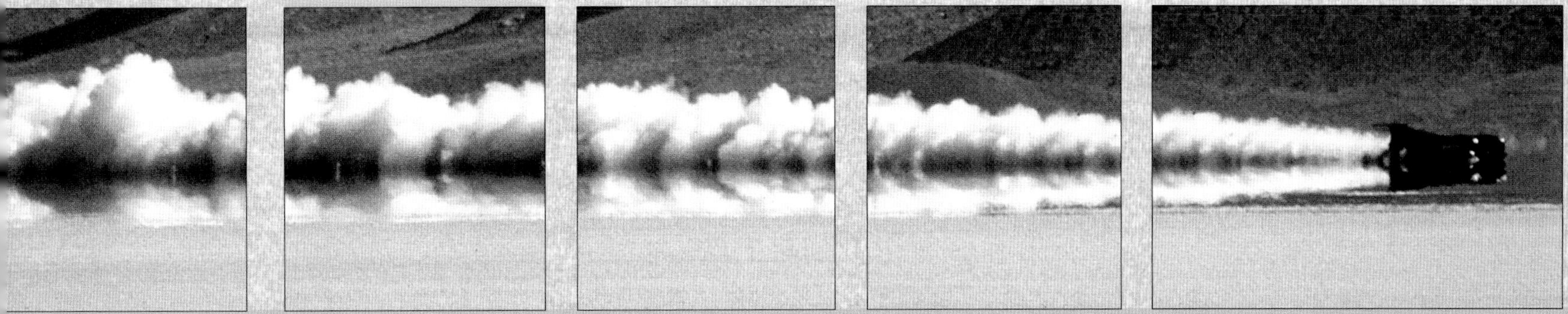

ThrustSSC (SuperSonicCar)
On 15 October 1997, fired on two Rolls-Royce Spey jet engines, the ThrustSSC was the first land vehicle to officially break the sound barrier at Mach 1. Driven by Andy Green of Britain, the ThrustSSC set a new land-speed record of 1,227.99 kph (763.035 mph) in the Black Rock Desert, USA. The open, flat surface of the unpopulated desert provides the perfect environment for land-speed attempts.

Classic cars

From luxury sports cars to family saloons, some vehicles go down in history for their stellar performance and fine styling. Car enthusiasts will pay a small fortune to purchase their favourite classic car, and will go to great lengths to restore it with reconditioned parts and maintain its original colour and form. While some classics such as the AC 428 were limited editions with very few cars produced, the Mustang "pony car" was the fastest-selling Ford ever, with more than two million of them sold between 1964 and 1970.

Pontiac Chieftain, 1949
0–96 kph (0–60 mph): 13 seconds
Number produced: N/A
Country of origin: USA

Land Rover Series 1, 1949
0–96 kph (0–60 mph): N/A
Number produced: 3,000
Country of origin: UK

Bentley R-Type Continental, 1952–55
0–96 kph (0–60 mph): 13.5 seconds
Number produced: 208
Country of origin: UK

Lancia Aurelia, 1954–56
0–96 kph (0–60 mph): 14.3 seconds
Number produced: 330
Country of origin: Italy

Mercedes 300SL Gullwing, 1954–57
0–96 kph (0–60 mph): 8.8 seconds
Number produced: 1,400
Country of origin: Germany

AC Ace Bristol, 1956–61
0–96 kph (0–60 mph): 9.1 seconds
Number produced: 463
Country of origin: UK

Chrysler New Yorker, 1957
0–96 kph (0–60 mph): 12.3 seconds
Number produced: 34,620
Country of origin: USA

Lotus Elite, 1957–63
0–96 kph (0–60 mph): 11.1 seconds
Number produced: 988
Country of origin: UK

Buick Limited Series 700 Rivera, 1958
0–96 kph (0–60 mph): 9.5 seconds
Number produced: 7,436
Country of origin: USA

Austin Healey Sprite Mk1, 1958–61
0–96 kph (0–60 mph): 20.5 seconds
Number produced: 38,999
Country of origin: UK

Ford Fairlane 500 Skyliner, 1959
0–96 kph (0–60 mph): 10.6 seconds
Number produced: 12,915
Country of origin: USA

Ferrari 250 GT SWB, 1959–62
0–96 kph (0–60 mph): 6.6 seconds
Number produced: 167
Country of origin: Italy

Porsche 356B, 1959–63
0–96 kph (0–60 mph): 10 seconds
Number produced: 30,963
Country of origin: Germany

Daimler SP250 Dart, 1959–64
0–96 kph (0–60 mph): 8.5 seconds
Number produced: 2,644
Country of origin: UK

NSU Sport Prinz, 1959–67
0–96 kph (0–60 mph): 27.7 seconds
Number produced: 20,831
Country of origin: Germany

Citroën DS Décapotable, 1960–71
0–96 kph (0–60 mph): 11.2 seconds
Number produced: 1,365
Country of origin: France

Jaguar E-type, 1961–74
0–96 kph (0–60 mph): 7.2 seconds
Number produced: 72,520
Country of origin: UK

Rolls-Royce Silver Cloud, 1962–65
0–96 kph (0–60 mph): 10.8 seconds
Number produced: 2,044
Country of origin: UK

MGB, 1962–80
0–96 kph (0–60 mph): 12.2 seconds
Number produced: 512,000
Country of origin: UK

Skoda Felicia, 1963
0–96 kph (0–60 mph): 27.5 seconds
Number produced: 15,864
Country of origin: Czech Republic

Chevrolet Corvette Stingray, 1963–67
0–96 kph (0–60 mph): 5.4 seconds
Number produced: 118,964
Country of origin: USA

Renault Alpine A110, 1963–77
0–96 kph (0–60 mph): 8.7 seconds
Number produced: 8,203
Country of origin: France

Lincoln Continental, 1964
0–96 kph (0–60 mph): 11 seconds
Number produced: 3,328
Country of origin: USA

Gordon Keeble GT, 1964–67
0–96 kph (0–60 mph): 7.5 seconds
Number produced: 104
Country of origin: UK

Ford Mustang, 1964–70
0–96 kph (0–60 mph): 6.1 seconds
Number produced: 2,077,826
Country of origin: USA

Datsun Fairlady, 1965–70
0–96 kph (0–60 mph): 13.3 seconds
Number produced: 40,000
Country of origin: Japan

Lamborghini Miura, 1966–72
0–96 kph (0–60 mph): 6.7 seconds
Number produced: 800
Country of origin: Italy

AC 428, 1966–73
0–96 kph (0–60 mph): 5.9 seconds
Number produced: 80
Country of origin: UK

Jensen Interceptor, 1966–76
0–96 kph (0–60 mph): 7.3 seconds
Number produced: 1,500
Country of origin: UK

Maserati Ghibli, 1967
0–96 kph (0–60 mph): 6.2 seconds
Number produced: 1,274
Country of origin: Italy

Chevrolet Camaro RS, 1967–70
0–96 kph (0–60 mph): 8.3 seconds
Number produced: 231,581
Country of origin: USA

Saab Sonett V4, 1968
0–96 kph (0–60 mph): 12 seconds
Number produced: 10,249
Country of origin: Sweden

Mercedes 280SL, 1968–71
0–96 kph (0–60 mph): 9.3 seconds
Number produced: 23,885
Country of origin: Germany

Alfa Romeo Spider, 1968–78
0–96 kph (0–60 mph): 11.2 seconds
Number produced: 7, 237
Country of origin: Italy

Triumph TR6, 1969–76
0–96 kph (0–60 mph): 29 seconds
Number produced: 94,619
Country of origin: UK

Porsche 911 Carrera RS, 1972–73
0–96 kph (0–60 mph): 5.6 seconds
Number produced: 1,580
Country of origin: Germany

Aston Martin V8, 1972–89
0–96 kph (0–60 mph): 6.2 seconds
Number produced: 2,842
Country of origin: UK

Peugeot 504, 1974
0–96 kph (0–60 mph): 11 seconds
Number produced: 977
Country of origin: France

Cadillac Seville, 1978
0–96 kph (0–60 mph): 11.5 seconds
Number produced: 56,985
Country of origin: USA

BMW M1, 1978–80
0–96 kph (0–60 mph): 5.4 seconds
Number produced: 457
Country of origin: Germany

Mazda RX7, 1978–85
0–96 kph (0–60 mph): 8.9 seconds
Number produced: 474,565
Country of origin: Japan

Delorean DMC12, 1979–82
0–96 kph (0–60 mph): 9.6 seconds
Number produced: 6,500
Country of origin: UK

Audi Quattro Sport, 1983–87
0–96 kph (0–60 mph): 4.8 seconds
Number produced: 80
Country of origin: Germany

Lancia Delta HF Integrale, 1986–92
0–96 kph (0–60 mph): 6.6 seconds
Number produced: N/A
Country of origin: Italy

Chevrolet Corvette ZR1, 1996
0–96 kph (0–60 mph): 3.9 seconds
Number produced: N/A
Country of origin: USA

Morgan Roadster V6, 2004–
0–96 kph (0–60 mph): 4.9 seconds
Number produced: N/A
Country of origin: UK

Modern legend

The majority of cars built today are designed by computers and constructed on fully automated assembly lines. But some luxury cars, such as this Morgan Roadster, are hand-built using traditional skills. The flowing lines and nostalgic look of the Morgan make it very popular, and customers have to join a waiting list of up to one year before they can own one.

When it gets to their turn, however, they can hand-pick the colour and all the fixtures and fittings of their custom-built sports car. The Morgan factory in England builds just 600 cars per year, and the average production time for one Morgan sports car is 23 days.

Room for two

Like all sports cars, the compact Morgan Roadster can only carry two people – the driver and one passenger. The seats are covered in leather, and the dashboard is carved from wood.

Engine power
Although the Morgan Roadster looks like a car from decades past, it contains a powerful and lightweight modern engine and can reach a top speed of 215 kph (134 mph).

At the back
A spare tyre is fitted to the rear of the car in case of a puncture. Also stored at the back of the car is a folded hood, which can be pulled over to make a roof when it rains.

People's car

In the 1930s, the German car engineer Ferdinand Porsche began work on a car that would revolutionize private transport. His aim was to produce a reliable, affordable vehicle that could carry a family of five at a speed of 100 kph (62 mph). Apart from its unique air-cooled rear engine, the resulting Volkswagen (German for "people's car") Type 1's most noticeable feature was its rounded, insect-like shape, which led to its nickname – "the Beetle". The Type 1 VW Beetle became one of the world's most popular cars. In its 65-year history, more than 21 million classic Beetles were produced.

Between 1934 and 1937, Porsche created several Beetle prototypes, including a car with a wooden frame and an aluminium body.

The original Type 1 Volkswagen Beetle was unveiled in 1938. Full-scale production of the Beetle began in 1945 in Wolfsburg, Germany.

Green VW Beetle taxis were a common sight in Mexico City until 2004, when all Mexican cabs were legally required to have four doors.

Beetle mania

■ The Beetle was not the only cult Volkswagen vehicle. Introduced in 1950, the VW Type 2 (better known as the camper van) was a hit with hippies.

■ In 1938, the classic Beetle's engine volume was 985 cc. By 2003, the Beetle's engine capacity had grown to 1.6 litres.

■ Most car engines are water-cooled. The Beetle's highly effective air cooling system had a surprise side effect: it gave the car its own distinctive sound!

■ The last original Beetle left the Volkswagen factory in Puebla, Mexico, on 30 July 2003. It is now in the Autostadt Museum, Wolfsburg.

1. The radiator contains water that helps to moderate the temperature of the engine.

2. Electrically operated, the fan is an additional method of cooling the car's engine.

3. The engine drives the wheels via the gearbox. Certain speeds relate to different gear ratios.

4. The body of the car is attached to connected steel tubes, which include the chassis rail.

5. Pedals are levers operated by the driver's feet to control the speed of the car.

6. A steering column shaft joins the steering wheel and the rack to which the wheels are attached.

7. The transmission tunnel is a metal container through which the gear lever connects the gearbox.

8. A driver-operated gearstick lever changes the gear according to the speed required.

9. The airbag housing contains an airbag used to reduce passengers' injuries in the event of a collision. The airbag is filled with gas that travels up the steering column.

10. The strong support legs that hold the roof of the car on to the rest of the body are called pillars.

11. The sunroof "window" in the car's roof can be opened to allow in extra light and fresh air.

12. An adjustable seat frame allows the driver or passenger to adjust the position and height of the seat.

13. The rear-door speaker transmits in-car entertainment to passengers sitting in the rear of the car.

14. The strong strap of the inertia reel seatbelt holds passengers in their seats in the event of a collision.

15. Electrically operated wires in the rear windscreen heat up the glass to defrost ice and prevent misting.

16. The headrest unit is designed to protect occupants' heads in the event of a high-speed impact.

17. The silencer reduces the sound made by the Beetle's engine exhaust pipe.

18. Above the silencer in the rear of the car, the boot floor offers an area to store luggage.

19. The rear bumper has been designed to cushion impact in the event of a collision.

In 1955, the one-millionth Volkswagen car, a gold-coloured Beetle, was produced in the company's factory in Wolfsburg, Germany.

Herbie, who first gained popularity in the 1968 Disney film *The Love Bug*, is a Beetle with a mind of its own and the ability to drive itself.

At Beetle festivals, such as Bug Jam in the UK, enthusiasts exhibit their cars, swap parts, and participate in drag races, Beetle against Beetle!

Volkswagen launched the New Beetle in 1998. Unlike the original Beetle, the New Beetle's engine is at the front instead of the rear.

On the road

When people load up their car and take a road trip, the excitement is not always in the destination, but in the journey itself. While aeroplanes make long-distance travel swift and convenient, for many, an open road provides a sense of freedom and adventure. In reality, the road trip is often zig-zagged with congested motorways that have been mapped and signposted long ago. Some road trips are famous, with travellers revelling in the nostalgia of the former Route 66 in the United States, and the spectacular rugged southern coastline of Australia's Great Ocean Road, to enjoying the epic adventure of driving from Alaska to Chile on the Pan-American Highway.

Circle, Alaska
22,160 km
(13,769 miles)

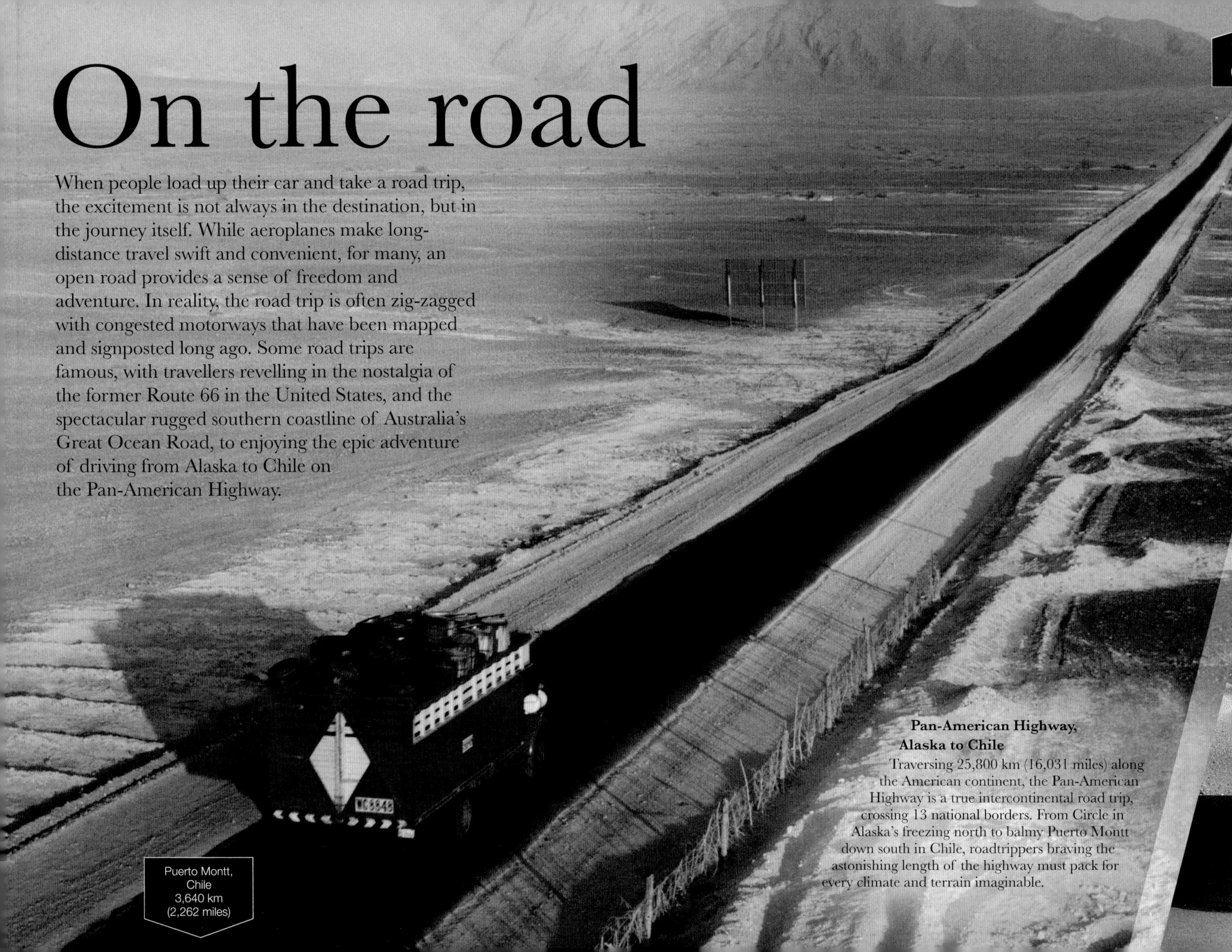

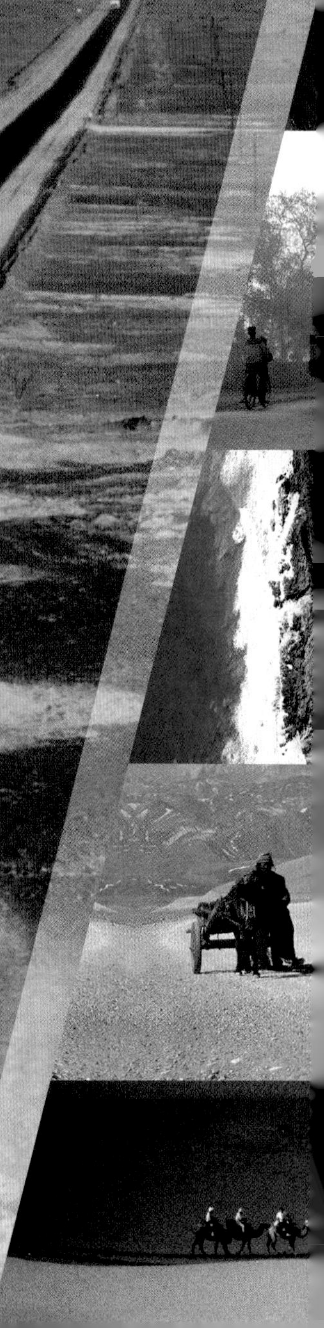

Pan-American Highway, Alaska to Chile

Traversing 25,800 km (16,031 miles) along the American continent, the Pan-American Highway is a true intercontinental road trip, crossing 13 national borders. From Circle in Alaska's freezing north to balmy Puerto Montt down south in Chile, roadtrippers braving the astonishing length of the highway must pack for every climate and terrain imaginable.

Puerto Montt,
Chile
3,640 km
(2,262 miles)

Dempster Highway, Canada

Length 741 km (460 miles)

From Dawson City to Inuvik, the Dempster Highway crosses rugged Canadian wilderness to the Arctic Circle. Passing mountain ranges, canyons, and waterfalls, the aurora borealis (Northern Lights) can be seen on the highway from February to April. In summer, it can be driven in 24-hour daylight.

Grand Trunk Road, India to Afghanistan

Length 2,600 km (1,615 miles)

Starting in Kolkata, India, crossing to Lahore, Pakistan, and ending in Kabul, Afghanistan, the 2,600-km (1,615-mile) Grand Trunk Road is historically known as "The Long Walk". With daredevil drivers, potholes, and roaming livestock, the Grand Trunk Road is a journey for the adventurous.

Great Ocean Road, Australia

Length 241 km (150 miles)

Skimming steep cliffs along Australia's southern coastline, the Great Ocean Road stretches from surf town Torquay in Victoria to Nelson near the South Australian border. The road winds past giant limestone stacks called the 12 Apostles, historical shipwrecks, and rainforests in the Otway Ranges.

Karakoram Highway, Pakistan to China

Length 1,300 km (807 miles)

Bridging Kashgar in China to Havelian in Pakistan, the Karakoram Highway was completed in 1978 in very hostile terrain. Passing the Karakoram, Pamir, and Himalayan mountain ranges, plus glaciers, green valleys, and desert, the highway carries travellers, tradespeople, yaks, and bactrian camels.

The Silk Road, Southern Asia

Length 8,046 km (4,999 miles)

With numerous interconnecting routes across southern Asia, the Silk Road was pivotal in the expansion of ancient civilizations in China, Egypt, India, and Rome. Spreading culture and international commerce, the Silk Road ceased functioning as a trade route in 1400.

Historical Route 66

Decommissioned as a highway in 1985, Route 66 is now a historical route, crossing from Chicago, Illinois, to Santa Monica, California. During the 1930s, poor farming families from the midwest travelled Route 66 hoping for better lives and job opportunities on the wealthier west coast.

Chicago
1,902 km
(1,182 miles)

SPEED LIMIT 45

Santa Monica
985 km
(612 miles)

Taxi!

Cabs conveniently transport passengers directly to their chosen location. They can be hailed in the street, queued for at a taxi stand, or hired by telephoning a dispatch centre. Taxis are often identified by their colour or livery, such as the famous yellow cabs in New York City, black cabs in London, and red cabs in urban Hong Kong. For people flagging a cab, a light on a taxi's roof indicates whether it is vacant or occupied.

Dodging Delhi's jams
More vehicles cram Delhi's streets than any other city in India. Visitors to Delhi tend to use taxis, while locals prefer to hire cheaper auto-rickshaws to get around. Taxis in Delhi are usually taken from a taxi stand or reserved via telephone, rather than being hailed in the street.

Cruising the Big Apple
In 1915, taxi fleet owner John D Hertz formed the "Yellow Cab Company" after discovering that yellow is the most visible colour from a distance. Today, more than 12,000 yellow cabs (known as "medallion taxis") roam the streets of New York City. With less than half of New Yorkers owning a car, it is estimated that more than 240 million passengers ride taxis across the city's five boroughs each year.

From Mayfair to Whitechapel
At the beginning of the 17th century, horse-drawn "hackney carriages" began providing taxi services in London. To drive one of London's famed black cabs today, potential drivers must pass a rigorous test called "The Knowledge". Applicants must memorize 320 routes and 25,000 streets within a 9.6-km (6-mile) radius of Charing Cross in the heart of London.

Tools of the trade

The taximeter, which was invented in 1891, enabled cab drivers to charge passengers for the exact distance travelled. Other taxi innovations were radio dispatch in the 1940s, and computerized dispatch in the 1980s. Increasingly, modern cabs are fitted with GPS (Global Positioning Systems). Using satellites to find the quickest routes for drivers, GPS technology (below) also assists cab companies in keeping better track of their fleets.

Cuban classics

Many of the cars in Cuba pre-date 1960, and have been sustained with spare parts or been mixed and matched to form hybrid cars. Classic 1950s American cars (such as Chevrolets and Oldsmobiles) cruise the main streets as *ruteros* – taxis running fixed routes. These taxis are often modified with extra seats welded to the car frame, creating room for at least eight passengers.

Taxi trivia

■ "Taxi" comes from the "taximeter" which measures the distance a cab travels. The word "cab" comes from "cabriolet", the name of 19th-century horse-drawn carriages used in Paris.

■ In 1636, the first taxi stand was established on the Strand in London. At that time, only 50 London carriages were permitted taxi licences.

■ In 1914, during World War I, 6,000 French troops were transported to the First Battle of the Marne via taxicabs.

■ Black cab drivers in London are renowned for having a particularly large hippocampus, which is a section of the brain related to learning and forming memories.

■ The first known female taxi driver drove a New York cab in 1925. In 2005, 407 of New York's 40,000 taxi drivers were women.

Intrepid Thai tuk-tuks

Small but speedy three-wheeled tuk-tuks weave through Thai city streets. They are fitted with tiny two-stroke engines and have handlebar steering. Passengers cram into the back seat behind the driver's cabin. Tuk-tuks are not fitted with meters, so passengers must first bargain with the driver for their fare.

Japanese silver service

Immaculately maintained, cabs in Japan are driven by drivers wearing white gloves. Fitted with GPS, Japanese cabs are technologically advanced. Drivers operate the rear left door via a button on their dashboard to let passengers in and out. This also prevents fingerprints marking the door!

Going by cable

San Francisco in California, USA, has the world's oldest cable car system. Cable cars are a type of light railway where the cars grip a moving cable.

Ups and downs

The first escalator was built in 1897 as a fairground attraction. They now feature in shopping centres and public buildings all around the world.

Urban movers

Moving lots of people quickly over short distances can present more of a challenge than long-distance travel. Town and city planners have to find efficient ways to move thousands of people from one place to another. The biggest crowds build up between transport hubs such as air, rail, and bus terminals.

When town and city planners are successful, people move in a steady flow – even during the peak times of the rush hour. Solutions for city travel have to be clean and sustainable, so that they do not contribute to urban pollution. Above all, they need to be as safe as possible for the users.

Rapid movement

In 2002, the Paris Metro unveiled the first *trottoir roulant rapide* (rapid-moving walkway). It carries around 110,000 pedestrians across busy Montparnasse station each day – a distance of 185 m (607 ft). Originally set at 11 kph (7 mph), the speed had to be lowered to 9 kph (6 mph) because so many passengers were falling over!

Travelling light
Trams are light railways. In the 1950s, many cities phased out trams in favour of buses. Now, new tram systems are being constructed, including the system built for the 2004 Olympics in Athens, Greece. Unlike buses, trams do not produce exhaust fumes, and their routes often bypass other road traffic.

Single track
As its name suggests, a monorail is a railway that has a single track. Compared to conventional railways, which run on two parallel rails, a monorail takes up less space. It is an attractive solution for elevated rail routes because it blocks out less sky. The monorail is also able to turn, climb, and descend faster than two-track railways.

Leaps and bounds
Not all urban travel is about finding a sensible route to work or school. Free-running (*le parkour*) began in the suburbs of Paris in the 1990s. It is an extreme sport that treats the city like an outsize obstacle course. Participants leap over rooftops and between buildings as smoothly and athletically as they can. It is a very dangerous activity, but the fluid movements can be exciting to watch.

The commuters

More than 2.5 million people travel on the Underground every day, crossing from one area of London to another. The Tube is a popular form of travel for Londoners, as well as the millions of tourists who visit the city every year.

Tatiana

Travelling on the London Underground is easy, according to Tatiana. "People on the Tube are always happy to help me lift the pram up and down stairs."

Jasper and Oliver

"We're taking the Tube to Heathrow Airport to go on holiday. The Tube is the fastest way to get around London."

Robin

"I travel to different Tube stations regularly to oversee the maintenance of the lifts and escalators. I find the Tube quick, clean, and very convenient."

Charlotta

"Travelling on the Tube is a great time to read or do a crossword," says Charlotta. "If I've forgotten a book, I love to people-watch."

Ben and Becky

"It is easy to visit London's famous landmarks on the Underground. We've just been to the Harrods department store to look at puppies."

Yumi

"The Underground is reliable and safe, and makes exploring London easy," says Yumi. From South Korea, she is on her way to college where she studies English.

Rush hour

The busiest time on the Underground is when people are travelling to and from work in the morning and evening. Trains run more frequently during these rush-hour periods.

Getting around

■ There are 275 Tube stations in London; 63 of them are in the central London area.
■ The Underground has 12 different lines. They are represented by different colours on network maps.

■ There are 976 million passenger journeys each year – an average of 2.67 million a day.
■ About 150,000 people enter London Underground stations every hour. The busiest station is Waterloo, which moves 46,000

people during the three-hour peak time in the morning – that is 255 people every minute.
■ Every year, 77.5 million passengers pass through Kings Cross St Pancras station.
■ The circular logo to represent the Tube,

called the roundel, first appeared in 1913.
■ To help travellers get around, the Tube map was designed in 1933 by Harry Beck. He was inspired by the shape of electrical circuits and his design is still the basis of today's map.

London Underground

Beneath the streets of London lies a vast network of train tunnels and stations. London Underground is the oldest metro system in the world, and one of the largest, with 408 km (253 miles) of track. Despite its name, it runs both underground and overland and is nicknamed "the Tube" by Londoners.

Steel and glass
One of the newest stations in the east of the city, Canary Wharf's modern architecture has won awards.

Going underground

Mazes of tunnels run beneath about 100 major cities of the world, with trains seamlessly transporting masses of commuters from place to place. Known variously as the subway, the metro, the Underground, or the Tube, underground railways are highly effective rapid-transit systems. Bypassing traffic jams and congestion in the streets above, these hidden public transport networks keep big cities on the move. Even at night, when most rail systems are shut, teams of engineers carry out maintenance work and safety checks to keep the rails running smoothly.

London
In 1863, the world's first underground railway opened in the United Kingdom, revolutionizing public transport. The Underground was steam-powered until the Northern Line introduced electric traction in 1890, making for a cleaner ride. With 12 busy lines, the Underground network now runs over 415 km (259 miles).

New York City
In the United States, the IRT (Interborough Rapid Transit) subway network opened in 1904 to ease the city's traffic problems. The 24-hour subway now has 277 of its 468 stations situated underground. Running every four minutes in rush hour, the subway shuttles an estimated 4.7 million passengers around New York City each workday.

○ **Mexico City** ○ **Toronto** ○ **Buenos Aires** ○ **Glasgow** ○ **Oslo** ○ **Berlin** ○ **Budapest**

Mexico City's metro is the world's cheapest, with a one-way fare costing two *pesos* (10p). During the metro's construction, ancient Aztec ruins and a 12,000-year-old woolly mammoth were discovered. Some of these artefacts are represented in station logos.

The Toronto Subway opened in 1954 as a U-shaped line, which has extended to four routes. The original subway was designed to replace the tram system that travelled the Canadian city's main thoroughfare. In peak hours, trains run every two to three minutes.

The oldest subway in South America is the first of Buenos Aires's subway lines, built in 1913. Known as the Subte, the underground network now has five routes through the Argentine capital, named alphabetically as A, B, C, D, and E lines. In all, there are 69 stations and 42.7 km (26.5 miles) of track.

Built in 1896, the subway in Glasgow is one of the oldest in the world. Its original trains were hauled on a continuous cable, but in 1935 the Scottish subway converted to electric trains. Completing a 10.4-km (6.5-mile) circuit, and with tangerine livery, locals have nicknamed their subway "Clockwork Orange".

In 1966, the overland train network in Oslo, Norway, was connected by tunnels to form the T-bane subway. In 2004, construction caused a tunnel on the busy Grorudbanen line to collapse. The tunnel was rebuilt in six months, relieving streets jammed with replacement buses.

Berlin has an extensive railway network, part of which, the U-Bahn, runs underground. In 1902, the U-Bahn line opened, with some of its stations situated underground. In the Cold War, when Berlin was divided into East and West Germany, the rail network was also split.

In 1896, Budapest was home to the first electric subway on the European mainland. Situated directly below the Hungarian city's street level and running a 5-km (3-mile) stretch, the original M1 line is just 2.75 m (9 ft) high and 6 m (20 ft) wide.

The workers

To keep such a busy transport system running efficiently, London Underground employs more than 12,500 people. Each person has a particular job to do, from driving trains and supervising platforms to handling emergencies.

Julian
"Meeting lots of people is the best thing about my job," says Julian, a customer services assistant. "And there is a great team spirit among the staff."

David
"The Emergency Response Unit deals with everything from signal failure to cutting trees on overland sections," explains manager David.

Ted
"People leave the strangest things on the Underground, and they can cause security alerts," says Ted, who works in the huge lost property department.

Said
"As duty station manager I run three stations and oversee 160 staff," says Said. "The Underground keeps London running."

Sue
"My job includes watching the platforms via CCTV cameras and making announcements to keep people safe and informed," Sue explains. "I like being in control!"

Anthony
"As a train driver on the Northern Line, I work in shifts of two to three hours, although sometimes I'll work longer. I have now worked for London Underground for 34 years!"

Tube trivia

- Each Underground train travels a total distance of 118,287 km (73,456 miles) every year.
- The average Underground train speed is 33 kph (20.5 mph).

- Today, the Underground is an electric railway. However, when the first trains ran on the system they were powered by steam.
- Of the network's 408 km (253 miles) of track, 45 per cent is underground.

- Many Tube stations were used as air-raid shelters during World War II.
- 410 escalators and 102 lifts transport passengers from surface to platform throughout the system.

- Hampstead station is the deepest station below street level, lying 58.5 m (192 ft) underground.
- The Underground is closed for five hours every night so that repairs can be made.

Going underground

Mazes of tunnels run beneath about 100 major cities of the world, with trains seamlessly transporting masses of commuters from place to place. Known variously as the subway, the metro, the Underground, or the Tube, underground railways are highly effective rapid-transit systems. Bypassing traffic jams and congestion in the streets above, these hidden public transport networks keep big cities on the move. Even at night, when most rail systems are shut, teams of engineers carry out maintenance work and safety checks to keep the rails running smoothly.

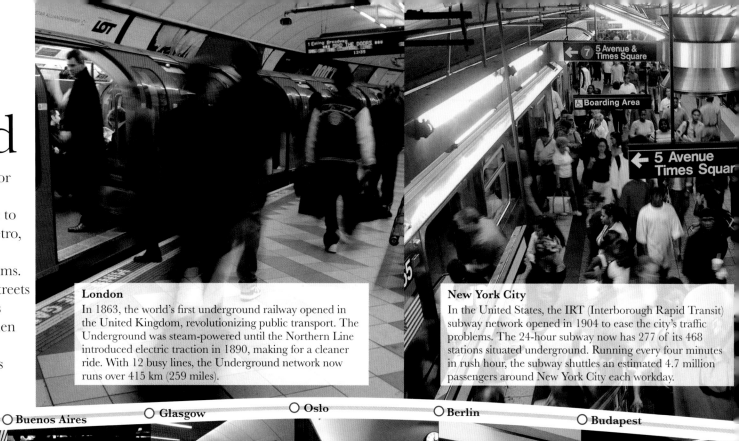

London
In 1863, the world's first underground railway opened in the United Kingdom, revolutionizing public transport. The Underground was steam-powered until the Northern Line introduced electric traction in 1890, making for a cleaner ride. With 12 busy lines, the Underground network now runs over 415 km (259 miles).

New York City
In the United States, the IRT (Interborough Rapid Transit) subway network opened in 1904 to ease the city's traffic problems. The 24-hour subway now has 277 of its 468 stations situated underground. Running every four minutes in rush hour, the subway shuttles an estimated 4.7 million passengers around New York City each workday.

○ **Mexico City** ○ **Toronto** ○ **Buenos Aires** ○ **Glasgow** ○ **Oslo** ○ **Berlin** ○ **Budapest**

Mexico City's metro is the world's cheapest, with a one-way fare costing two *pesos* (10p). During the metro's construction, ancient Aztec ruins and a 12,000-year-old woolly mammoth were discovered. Some of these artefacts are represented in station logos.

The Toronto Subway opened in 1954 as a U-shaped line, which has extended to four routes. The original subway was designed to replace the tram system that travelled the Canadian city's main thoroughfare. In peak hours, trains run every two to three minutes.

The oldest subway in South America is the first of Buenos Aires's subway lines, built in 1913. Known as the Subte, the underground network now has five routes through the Argentine capital, named alphabetically as A, B, C, D, and E lines. In all, there are 69 stations and 42.7 km (26.5 miles) of track.

Built in 1896, the subway in Glasgow is one of the oldest in the world. Its original trains were hauled on a continuous cable, but in 1935 the Scottish subway converted to electric trains. Completing a 10.4-km (6.5-mile) circuit, and with tangerine livery, locals have nicknamed their subway "Clockwork Orange".

In 1966, the overland train network in Oslo, Norway, was connected by tunnels to form the T-bane subway. In 2004, construction caused a tunnel on the busy Grorudbanen line to collapse. The tunnel was rebuilt in six months, relieving streets jammed with replacement buses.

Berlin has an extensive railway network, part of which, the U-Bahn, runs underground. In 1902, the U-Bahn line opened, with some of its stations situated underground. In the Cold War, when Berlin was divided into East and West Germany, the rail network was also split.

In 1896, Budapest was home to the first electric subway on the European mainland. Situated directly below the Hungarian city's street level and running a 5-km (3-mile) stretch, the original M1 line is just 2.75 m (9 ft) high and 6 m (20 ft) wide.

Tokyo

The first Tokyo subway line opened in 1927 and ran just 2.2 km (1.4 miles) between Ueno and Asakusa. Today, the Japanese city has a thriving subway with 12 busy lines. During rush hour, conductors jam passengers onto packed carriages. Some passengers sleep during their commute, setting their mobile phone alarms to wake them at their station.

Paris

In France, Paris's subway pioneered the name the "Métro" when it was built in 1900. In 1956, quieter and fast-accelerating rubber-tyred trains – developed by French companies Michelin and Renault – were introduced. Dubbed the "Meteor" when it opened in 1998, the Métro's newest line, Ligne 14, is fully automated.

Moscow

Built in 1935 during Soviet rule, the metro in Moscow has grand marble stations with art, chandeliers, and mosaics. Carrying eight to nine million passengers every day, the Russian subway is the world's busiest. Male staff announce trains running into the city, while female announcers cover those travelling out of Moscow.

○ St Petersburg   ○ Cairo   ○ Kolkata   ○ Singapore   ○ Hong Kong   ○ Pyongyang   ○ Melbourne

The metro in St Petersburg, Russia, is 112 km (70 miles) long and has 61 stations. Many of these lay as deep as 120 m (394 ft) beneath street level. In the rush hour, trains pass every 95 seconds.

In 1987, the Cairo Metro was the first subway to be built on the African continent. There are two lines, with a third line planned to connect the Egyptian city centre to the outlying Cairo airport.

India's first subway, the Kolkata Metro Railway, was built in 1984. It runs for 16.5 km (10 miles), with 17 stations along the route. Each platform is 160 m (525 ft) long.

Platform screen doors help to control the climate of Singapore's modern subway, and also protect its commuters. In 2003, automated, driverless trains were introduced.

Of Hong Kong's 50 train stations, 34 are situated underground. Two of the subway lines cross Hong Kong Harbour to service the suburb of Kowloon on the Chinese mainland.

In Pyongyang, North Korea, 17 metro stations lay up to 100 m (328 ft) underground, doubling as nuclear bunkers. The stations have political rather than geographical names.

The rail network in Melbourne is overland, but most suburban trains run an underground circuit called the City Loop. Built in 1984, three subway stations on the Loop service the Australian city's central business district.

Line art

Each of the underground railway systems in cities around the world has its own distinctive design. Whether catching the subway in New York City or the T-bana in Stockholm, colourful signs at street level provide clear directions to the nearest station. The visual display continues underground, with illuminated maps and ticket machines providing information, and sculptures and paintings that make the journey more pleasant.

Denmark: Copenhagen Metro

Singapore: Singapore Metro

Czech Republic: Prague Metro

Russia: Moscow Metro

The Netherlands: Rotterdam Metro

Hong Kong: Hong Kong Metro

Japan: Tokyo Metro

Thailand: Bangkok Metro

Italy: Rome Metro

Austria: Vienna U-Bahn

Belgium: Brussels Metro

Portugal: Lisbon Metro

Japan: Osaka Metro

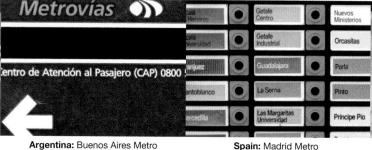

Argentina: Buenos Aires Metro

Spain: Madrid Metro

Austria: Salzburg U-Bahn

Sweden: Stockholm T-bana

USA: Los Angeles Subway

UK: London Underground

Spain: Barcelona Metro

Greece: Athens Metro

China: Pyongyang Metro

Italy: Naples Metro

Russia: St Petersburg Metro

China: Guangzhou Metro

China: Shanghai Metro

Poland: Warsaw Metro

Egypt: Cairo Metro

Mexico: Mexico City Metro

China: Beijing Subway

USA: New York Subway

France: Paris Metro

Germany: Berlin U-Bahn

Spain: Barcelona Metro

Spain: Valencia Metro

Easy reading

Subway maps have to be clear and easy to read. Most do not accurately represent distances between stations on the ground but instead show the position of the stations in relation to each other on particular lines. Some, like these examples from Beijing, China, and Paris, France, are overlaid on an overground map of the city with streets, rivers, and other features marked on them. You can now download subway maps that can be viewed on a personal MP3 player.

First to set foot

12 October 1492

The Genoese explorer Christopher Columbus was the first European to set foot on American soil. His fleet landed at a place Columbus called San Salvador. Experts believe this was one of the Bahamas, probably Samana Cay island.

14 December 1911

The first people to reach the geographic South Pole were part of an expedition led by the Norwegian explorer Roald Amundsen. A British team, led by Robert Falcon Scott, arrived a month later but did not survive.

29 May 1953

Edmund Hillary of New Zealand and Sherpa Tenzing Norgay of Nepal were the first to reach the peak of Everest. The mountain is the world's tallest, rising 8,850 m (29,035 ft) above sea level. It is part of the towering Himalayan chain.

19 April 1968

American Ralph Plaisted was the first person to undisputedly set foot on the geographic North Pole. Fellow American Robert Peary believed that he reached it on 6 April 1909, but experts think he was probably a few kilometres away.

One small step

The first footprints on the Moon were made on 21 July 1969 by American astronaut Neil Armstrong, commander of the *Apollo 11* space mission. Armstrong recognized that it was a historic, symbolic moment. As he stepped out of the *Eagle* landing craft, he announced "That's one small step for man, one giant leap for mankind." The prints from Armstrong's moon boots are still there, and so are the prints of other astronauts who explored the lunar surface. That is because there is no wind on the Moon to blow them away.

First impressions

A footprint is an extraordinary thing. It is evidence of human life and human traffic. Most footprints are short-lived – they disappear as snow melts or mud is washed away. Footprints last only in extraordinary circumstances, such as the eruption of a volcano or the weatherless conditions of the Moon. When footprints are preserved, they function as talismans, powerful symbols of how humankind as a whole strives, adapts, and survives. In 2003, archaeologists working on the Roccamonfina volcano near Naples, southern Italy, found three tracks of footprints preserved in volcanic ash. Made 385,000 to 325,000 years ago, the fossilized prints are the oldest-known *Homo* (human) footprints from an ancient civilization.

Prehistoric prints

The earliest-known samples of hominid (prehuman) footprints were discovered in 1976 in Laetoli, Tanzania. These footprints were made 3.6 million years ago by two upright-walking hominids known as *Australopithecus afarensis*. By examining the trails, experts have worked out that one of the track-makers was large, while the other was small. Some experts argue that the impressions indicate that one of the creatures had an infant resting on its hip. The prehistoric tracks were made in volcanic ash, which became a cement-like substance when wet from rain. Then, following another violent volcanic eruption, the footsteps were preserved in a final layer of ash.

On foot

From planes and trains to buses and bikes, there are many forms of transport to get us from place to place, but with all our modern forms of transport, some journeys on Earth can only be undertaken on foot, such as the 8,850-m (29,035-ft) climb to the summit of the world's highest mountain, Mount Everest. Walking is our oldest method of getting around, and sometimes it is simply quicker and more pleasurable to use our feet.

Peak of fitness

Climbing a great mountain is an immense achievement and a perilous adventure. Potential disaster always looms, from the possibility of altitude sickness, hypothermia, and frostbite, to changeable weather conditions, falling rocks, and avalanches. Mountaineers must have the energy to scale the mountain while carrying all of their climbing tools, camping equipment, and food.

Walking wonders

■ In New York City, an estimated total of 10,300 km (6,400 miles) of footpath provides pedestrians access all over the city.

■ American David Kunst was the first person to walk around the world. The journey took over four years, and Kunst wore out 21 pairs of shoes crossing four continents and covering 23,250 km (14,447 miles).

■ When mountaineers climb to an altitude of more than 8,000 m (26,247 ft), the reduced oxygen levels decrease their mental performance by 70 per cent.

■ In the United Kingdom, the average person walks a total of 322 km (200 miles) each year. Individual journeys are an average distance of 1 km (0.6 miles).

■ Between April 1931 and October 1932, Plennie Wingo walked backwards from California, USA, to Istanbul, Turkey. His journey covered 12,875 km (8,000 miles).

Taking the high route

Throughout the Alps, high-level footpaths known as *Via Ferrata* or *Klettersteig* are fitted with cables, steel ladders, and suspension bridges. Equipped with safety equipment, such as helmets, ropes, and harnesses, hikers can use the paths to reach high pinnacles that would otherwise require advanced rock-climbing skills.

Heavy crowds

When thousands of people gather to walk together, the sea of faces they create is an amazing sight! There are many reasons why people converge to walk in massive groups, from protests and rallies, to cultural parades and religious pilgrimages, such as this gathering in Tibet.

City traffic

In congested cities, the quickest way to travel short distances is usually on foot. The world's busiest pedestrian crossing is Hachiko Crossing in Tokyo, Japan. It is estimated that between two to three million people walk across it each day. Every three minutes, road traffic is stopped to make way for the flood of pedestrians.

Pedal power

Bicycles have come a long way since the first "boneshakers" rattled along cobblestone streets and unpaved roads in the mid-1800s. Today's bicycles are built in all shapes and sizes to suit all sorts of terrains, from city streets to country tracks. Most bicycles have added gears and suspension to provide a more comfortable ride. Riding a bicycle is a cheap and efficient means of transport, and is especially convenient when used to cover short distances, or to tour and explore at an easy pace. Cycling is also a popular sport, with riders racing either cross-country or on purpose-built tracks called velodromes.

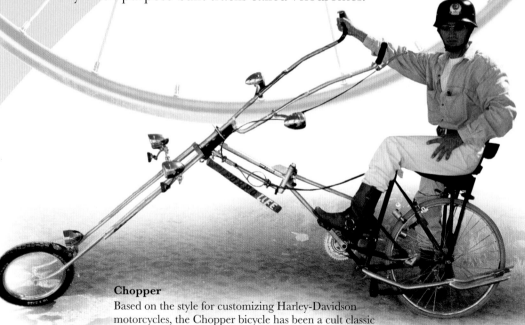

Chopper
Based on the style for customizing Harley-Davidson motorcycles, the Chopper bicycle has been a cult classic since the 1970s. It has different-sized wheels and high-rise handlebars. One of its most distinctive features is the long, padded seat with a backrest, which provides just enough room for a passenger.

Monowheel
This odd-looking vehicle, designed in 2000 by Chinese inventor Li Yongli, is a monowheel. Like a unicycle, a monowheel has just one wheel. The difference is that the rider sits inside the rim of the wheel to control the vehicle. The main wheel is propelled by a series of smaller, pedal-driven wheels.

Unicycle
Popular with clowns, jugglers, trapeze artists, and stunt performers, a unicycle has just one wheel. Unicycles with extra-tall seat posts are known as "giraffes". It takes practice and balance to be a unicyclist.

Trishaw
A three-wheeled rickshaw, or trishaw, uses pedal power to transport people or goods. This Vietnamese man is driving his family, but trishaws also operate as taxis in southern Asian cities.

Cruiser
A cruiser is built for maximum riding comfort, with laid-back handlebars, and wide, smooth tyres. It also has a padded seat and few or no gears. Some cruisers are specifically built for beach-side rides.

Recumbent bicycle
A rider on a recumbent bike sits back or lies down. Riding in this reclining position is more comfortable than riding a conventional upright bicycle, and places less strain on the back and joints.

Folding bicycle
Many bike manufacturers produce models that fold up. A folding bike takes up less storage space than a conventional one, and it can be carried easily for part of a journey, in a car or on public transport.

Tandem
Multi-bicycles carry more than one rider. The two-person tandem is the most common. The challenge for tandem riders is to synchronize their effort, especially if they have different levels of ability.

Racing bicycle
With its lightweight frame, raised seat, dropped handlebars, and narrow, high-pressure tyres, a racing bike is super fast. Time-trial bikes like this one have many aerodynamic features to increase speed.

Mountain bicycle
Designed for off-road cycling on tough terrains, mountain bikes have a strong frame, added suspension, and wide, treaded tyres. Some mountain bikes have up to 27 gears.

Classic bicycle
There are more than 1,000 million bikes in the world, and most are standard models for everyday use. Popular accessories include a basket to carry goods, and a bell to warn people that the bicycle is approaching.

BMX
Developed for dirt-track racing, BMX (short for "bicycle motocross") bicycles are also ridden freestyle – performing wheelies, jumps, and other tricks. BMX bikes have relatively small wheels – usually 50 cm (20 in) across. Their knobby tyres give them an excellent grip on sand, dirt, and slopes.

Mountain bike

With high traction tyres, a large rounded frame, and added suspension, mountain bikes, such as the Scott Genius RC-10, are built tough to ride through forests and bushland, trek rocky plains, or slide down steep gravel trails. The first mountain bikes were created in the 1970s by off-road biking enthusiasts in California, USA. With dirt motorbikes as their inspiration, they modified 1940s Schwinn bicycles, adding deep-treaded tyres and strong brakes. Today, around eight out of 10 bicycles sold are mountain bikes, yet only 10 to 20 per cent of these are actually ridden off-road.

Smooth steering

The front wheel on a mountain bike is connected to the frame by forks, which also enable the rider to steer. The quality of the forks directly affects the handling of the mountain bike. TheTerraLogic™ forks on the Scott Genius RC-10 can be adjusted to alter the level of suspension. The forks are designed to be stiff when riding a smooth road, but pump into action when riding over rough ground.

Spring suspension

Good suspension provides mountain bikers with a smoother ride on uneven terrain. Inside the forks, spring-loaded shock absorbers help soften the impact from the ground.

❶ Force from a bump pushes the slider up.

❷ Damping mechanism is activated allowing the oil to pass through a hole. This controls the speed the fork reacts to bumps.

❸ Air is compressed by a piston moving up the stanchion absorbing the force of the bump.

❹ Spring helps ease the slider as it returns to its starting position.

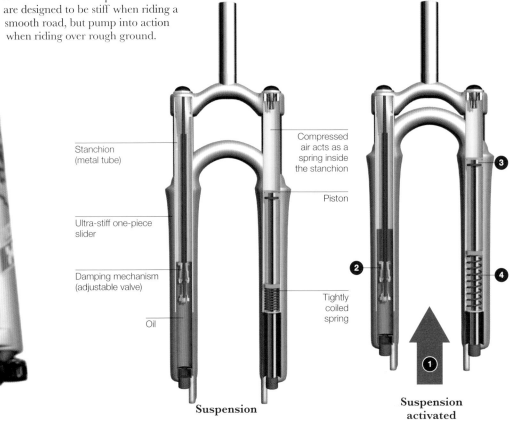

Stanchion (metal tube)

Ultra-stiff one-piece slider

Damping mechanism (adjustable valve)

Oil

Compressed air acts as a spring inside the stanchion

Piston

Tightly coiled spring

Suspension

Suspension activated

A champion ride

The Scott Genius RC-10 is popular with serious riders and athletes. On the Genius's release in 2003, the bike's success was sealed when racer Thomas Frischknecht rode a Genius to win the marathon distance in the Mountain Bike World Championships in Lugano, Italy.

Frame anatomy

The triangle is the strongest geometric shape, able to withstand extreme pressure. Two triangles form the standard diamond bike frame. Mountain bike frames are modified to accommodate suspension.

Pedal power

When a rider presses a lever on the handlebar, derailleur gears send the bike chain to "derail" across a series of sprockets into another gear. Gears ease the burden placed on the rider. For example, when climbing hills in a low gear, the rider must pedal more, but can put less pressure on the pedals than if they are riding in a higher gear. The Scott Genius RC-10 gives riders the choice of 27 gears.

Seat

Stem

Head tube

Gear cable

Brake hose

Top tube

Seat tube

Deep tread tyre

Down tube

Forks

Seat stays

Chain stays

Wheel rim

Wheel spoke

SCOTT

Chain

Tour de France

The Tour de France is the world's most famous bicycle race. The route of the race changes annually, traversing France and sometimes entering other European countries. Every July, spectators cheer for their cycling heroes along country roads to Paris's magnificent avenue, the Champs-Élysées. The three-week race is broken into around 20 stages, with 21 teams of nine cyclists competing for the prized *maillot jaune* (yellow jersey).

Tough terrain

Alpe d'Huez is infamous for being an especially long and steep Alpine stage, with an altitude of 1,860 m (6,102 ft). Climbing across 13.9 km (8.6 miles) at a steep gradient, the imposing mountain regularly features as an arduous day in the Tour.

Time trials

Strategically spread across the Tour, three or four time trials see teams and individuals competing against the clock for the fastest race times. Time trials are the only part of the Tour where cyclists are allowed to use aerodynamically designed helmets and handlebars. This streamlined equipment helps cyclists to reach top speeds.

Winning stages

Cyclists' times are accumulated on a system called the General Classification. The rider ranked first on the General Classification after the final stage of the Tour is the overall winner. If a rider is awarded two jerseys at the same time, he will wear the most prestigious jersey.

Racing hazards

While bad weather is one hazard that cyclists must contend with, there is also interference from supporters lining the route. Some fans slap riders on the back, wave flags close to the bicycles, throw water, or, most dangerously, leap on to the track. Serious accidents can also occur when cyclists become tangled with one another at high speeds.

Riding in packs

The *peloton* is the French term used to describe the main group of cyclists riding together. Team members work together to set the pace of the *peloton*. The rider who is at the front of the pack will spend several seconds using 100 per cent of his pedalling ability until another team member relieves him and takes over the lead.

Best young rider
The *maillot blanc* (white jersey) is awarded to the best young rider. The rider must be aged under 25 on 1 January of the year of the Tour.

King of the mountains
The *maillot à pois rouge* (white jersey with red polka dots) is awarded to the cyclist who is the best climber across the Tour's mountain stages.

Overall leader
The *maillot jaune* (yellow jersey) is awarded to the rider who accumulates the lowest times in the race. The final overall leader receives this jersey at the podium.

Points leader
The *maillot vert* (green jersey) is awarded to the rider who wins the most points across various stages of the Tour. Good sprinters tend to win this jersey.

City cycling

With urban roads becoming more and more congested, it is little wonder that the number of bicycle commuters is rising. Most use their bikes to travel to and from work, while a few are in the saddle all day as part of their job. The bicycle has many advantages for the city traveller – it costs nothing to run or park, is pollution-free, and it keeps riders fit. Cyclists can outpace cars and buses on short journeys because they can avoid traffic jams. Some cities, such as Amsterdam in the Netherlands, have introduced bike-friendly traffic measures to encourage commuters to cycle to work.

Green for go!

There are a variety of road signs and traffic measures in place to help cyclists. This traffic light signal means that only bikes can go. After a short time the light turns completely green so that all road traffic facing it can advance. It gives cyclists a useful head start in crossing complicated road junctions.

Lane-free road

In Vietnam, as in many Asian countries, far more peop travel by bicycle than in cars, buses, or trucks. There are n cycle lanes, but often there are no road markings for ar kind of traffic. People make their way around the city a best they can. Brakes and a loud horn or bell are essentia

In the fast lane

Amsterdam has 284 km (176 miles) of cycle lanes. Most experts think that cycle-only lanes make city cycling safer. They reduce the risk of drivers coming too close and make cyclists less likely to ride on the footpath, where they are a danger to pedestrians.

Saving lives

London is one of many cities that is pioneering the use of paramedic bike teams. These paramedics save lives because they can reach the scene of an emergency quickly. Carrying a range of first-aid equipment and drugs, the bicycle paramedic assesses and stabilizes the patient before an ambulance arrives.

In the post

Soon after the bicycle was invented, it was adopted for delivering mail. In 1896, the British post office bought 100 bicycles. Today, bikes are standard-issue for postal workers around the world, from Japan to the USA. The Swiss postal service alone owns more than 3,700 delivery bikes.

Bike patrol

Many police forces have bicycle patrol units. They can cover large areas without getting caught in traffic, which makes them more efficient for patrols or pursuing suspects. Police officers patrolling on bicycles are easy to approach, which helps them to build good relationships in the community.

Speedy delivery

In India, cycle rickshaws are often used to transport goods. The rickshaws are cheaper than using a delivery van, and do not add to the air and noise pollution. However, goods can be damaged if there are heavy rains. Some types of rickshaws have electric motors to help drivers turn the pedals.

Dropped handlebars enable more steering positions than upright handlebars.

Shoe straps help the rider grip the pedal.

This bike has one single, fixed gear.

Sending messages

Bike messengers carry packages to all parts of New York City, delivering anything from important business documents to gifts. Some bike messengers are so fast and efficient that they can deliver up to 40 packages in one working day.

Marathon

Running a marathon is an epic feat of human endurance, requiring peak physical condition and mental stamina. To complete the arduous 42.195-km (26.2-mile) course, many runners adopt a six-month training schedule involving five or six distance runs each week. Around the world, there are more than 800 marathons held each year. Some marathons, such as those in New York City and London, are so popular that amateur runners must first enter a ballot or lottery system for an opportunity to run in the race.

Water and sugary energy drinks keep runners hydrated.

Wraparound sunglasses cut out the sun's glare and dangerous ultraviolet rays.

Stopwatches motivate runners to improve on their best running times.

Registration numbers are used to identify runners.

Core-strength exercises, such as stomach crunches, give runners added stamina.

High-tech materials draw sweat away from the skin.

Burning up

During a marathon, an athlete's liver and muscles convert carbohydrates into a fast-burning energy called glycogen. Glycogen lasts around 32 km (20 miles) before the body burns its fat stores. Runners can then become fatigued, which is known as "hitting the wall".

Leg-strengthening exercises enable runners to move more efficiently.

Soft, lightweight racing shoes help marathon runners last the distance.

An electronic timing chip is clipped on to the shoe to record official running time.

Start times are staggered so elite runners are not held up by amateur athletes.

Water stands line the route to help runners avoid dehydration.

Runners drink diluted sports gels and special drinks to build up energy levels.

Half-marathon races are a good way to train for a full marathon.

| mile 01 (1.6 km) | mile 02 (3.2 km) | mile 03 (4.8 km) | mile 04 (6.4 km) | mile 05 (8 km) | mile 06 (9.6 km) | mile 07 (11.3 km) | mile 08 (12.9 km) | mile 09 (14.5 km) | mile 10 (16 km) | mile 11 (17.7 km) | mile 12 (19.3 km) | mile 13 (20.9 km) |

Famous marathons

The world's five most prestigious city marathons are in Berlin, Boston, Chicago, London, and New York City. The biggest marathons are in New York and London. In 2005, 36,856 runners completed the New York Marathon, while 35,260 runners finished London's race.

Race for everyone

On 21 April 1975, the Boston Marathon was the first major marathon to include a wheelchair division. Today's marathons are open to any athlete up to the challenge, whether they are able-bodied or have a disability.

Many runners hit "the wall" when energy levels are at a low.

The name "marathon" comes from an Ancient Greek legend in which a soldier ran 34.5 km (21.4 miles) from the Battle of Marathon to Athens.

The marathon length was fixed at the 1908 London Olympics, with the start line moved back to give the British royal family a better view.

| mile 14 (22.5 km) | mile 15 (24.1 km) | mile 16 (25.7 km) | mile 17 (27.3 km) | mile 18 (28.9 km) | mile 19 (30.6 km) | mile 20 (32.2 km) | mile 21 (33.8 km) | mile 22 (35.4 km) | mile 23 (37 km) | mile 24 (38.6 km) | mile 25 (40.2 km) | mile 26.2 (42.195 km) |

Extreme!

Pushing skills to the limit, adrenaline-pumped sports involving speed and thrill-seeking are often dubbed "extreme". Since the 1980s, skateboarding has become a hugely popular recreational activity for young people. Along with skateboarding, extreme sports such as freestyle motocross, inline skating, kite skating, and BMX feature in the Gravity Games and other professional tournaments around the world. Snowboarding is the first extreme sport to become an Olympic event, debuting in the 1998 Winter Olympics in Nagano, Japan.

Riding high

A vert ramp is a structure where skateboarders, inline skaters, and BMX riders perform aerial tricks. The flat floor gradually forms a U-shape ending in two vertical walls. The ramps are usually more than 3 m (10 ft) tall, with vertical sections of wall measuring up to 1 m (3 ft).

Tricks and kicks

In 1978, 15-year-old Alan Gelfand invented skateboarding's most famous trick, the "ollie". Many tricks, such as this kickflip (pictured), stem from the ollie. Skaters perform an ollie by using their back foot to snap down hard on the tail of the skateboard, while sliding their front foot forwards. Seemingly defying gravity, the board can be manoeuvred by the skater mid-flight.

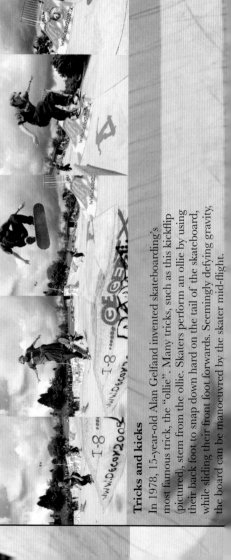

Kite skating

Propelled along by wind-powered kites, kite skaters require wide surfaces such as beaches, empty car parks, or open fields to perform their sport. As kites are involved, it is important that both the air and ground space are not obstructed. Some kite skaters choose to ride four-wheeled mountain boards (pictured), while others use off-road inline skates, fitted with large, high-traction wheels.

Inline skating

Using skates fitted with four or five wheels positioned in a single line, inline skaters ride on many of the same terrains as skateboarders. "Aggressive skating" is a type of inline street skating in which skaters perform dramatic jumps and tricks, such as grinding (riding on handrails down stairs). Some people inline skate without brakes, while others use a stop located on the heel of one skate.

Street luge

Torpedoing down steep mountain roads in a horizontal position, street luge racers can reach high speeds of 130 kph (81 mph). Riders must wear motorcycle helmets and leather safety gear for protection. Street luge boards are sometimes custom-made, built from carbon fibre, steel, wood, or aluminium. Riders steer their luge boards by leaning their bodies to the left or right.

Snowboarding

"Freestyle" is one of the most popular forms of snowboarding, where riders perform tricks similar to those done on skateboards. Some ski fields have designated areas with jumps for boarders. As with skateboarding, snowboarders who place their right foot forward on the board are known as "goofy", while "regular" riders ride with their left foot to the front.

Off the kerb

Whether they are riding on inline skates or a skateboard, many street skaters use public facilities to perform their tricks, such as kerbs, steps, and handrails. Urban skate parks have these facilities purpose-built for street skaters in a safer environment.

Snow motion

Snow and ice can bring chaos to the roads, even in parts of the world that are used to severe weather conditions. The principal challenge is to stay upright! Wheels are not designed for travelling over a surface that has almost no friction. They need help in the form of treaded tyres or snow chains. On motorways and main roads, there are usually measures to clear the snow altogether, such as gritting or snowploughs. Skis, sleds, and motorized snowmobiles are a practical way to travel over snow, as they rest upon runners that simply slide across the slippery surface.

Tyre chains
In mountainous, snowy areas, such as the Alps or the Rockies, cars may have to use snow chains to drive in the icy conditions. These chains are fitted on the wheels and help to prevent dangerous skidding. They are especially useful in the mountains, where roads have tight turns that can be hidden by huge snowdrifts.

Driving on ice
Four-wheel-drive vehicles have more traction on ice than cars in which only the front wheels are powered, but all drivers can minimize skidding. To slow down, drivers should ease pressure off the accelerator. Braking hard can result in loss of control.

Clearing roads
Spreading grit (usually rock salt) on main roads and busy footpaths is common practice wherever freezing conditions are forecast. The salt helps ice and snow to melt more quickly and gives tyres something to grip in the meantime. In serious blizzards, snowploughs have to clear the roads.

Snowshoes
Strapped over ordinary shoes, snowshoes help people to walk through snow without slipping or sinking. There is evidence that people have made them for thousands of years. The racket-shaped frame that surrounds a lattice of leather or string is designed not to collect snow.

Travelling by sled
Traditionally, people living in the Arctic cross snowy terrain by sled – vehicles that slide along ski-like runners rather than rolling on wheels. Sleds are made of wood and are usually pulled along by reindeer or huskies (a breed of dog). They can transport goods or people over the ice at high speeds.

City skiing
During the blizzard of 2003, some New Yorkers moved around the city on skis. The storm was a freak event but in some places, such as Scandinavian countries, skiing is still used as a practical means of travel. Cross-country skiing originated in Norway in the 1800s. Early skis were made of wood, while today's are usually fibreglass.

Snowmobile

Motorized sleds, called snowmobiles, are especially popular in the far north of the USA and Canada, where snow lies on the ground for many months of the year. They have skis, a petrol engine, and can travel across ice at speeds of 72 kph (45 mph).

340 Indy

POLA

IFS

Emergency!

"Emergency!" is written in reverse on medical response vehicles, so drivers can see the word correctly in their rear-view mirrors and know to pull over, allowing them to pass. Many emergency services vehicles have flashing lights and a loud siren to warn people in the vicinity that their journey is urgent. These public service teams include police, paramedics, and firefighters. Depending on the location of the situation and the type of emergency reported, response teams can arrive at the scene in anything from a huge truck to a sports car.

Arriving in style
Traffic police in Italy have use of a high-speed Lamborghini car. The equipment inside the vehicle includes direct connection to police databases, technology to record violations, and a scanner for number plate recognition.

Access all areas
Smart cars are used by police in countries such as the Czech Republic and UK. These compact cars have room for a police officer and emergency equipment, and are small enough to safely zip around city streets.

Speedy service
Motorbike ambulances can reach emergency situations much faster than their van counterparts. As well as weaving through traffic jams, motorbikes save time by stopping at the scene instead of parking somewhere first.

Mobile medication
Larger ambulances, such as this Japanese camper van, have a driver and at least one paramedic at every emergency. These vehicles have the equipment to stabilize a sick or injured patient's condition during the trip to hospital.

First ambulances: Horse-drawn ambulances during the American Civil War, 1861–65   **Largest ambulance service:** London, UK, with 1.5 million patients a year   **Biggest ambulance:** 18-m- (59-ft-) long Alligator Jumbulances, UK

Fire extinguishers
When a blaze is reported, a fire engine is sent from an emergency dispatch centre to put out the flames. Fire trucks, such as this one in Indiana, USA, have a large on-board water supply, which can be pumped through hoses managed by the firefighters. Fire engines also carry ladders, axes, and breathing apparatus.

KOKOMO FIRE DEPT.

Largest volunteer ambulance service: Abdul Sattar Edhi, Pakistan, with 500 ambulances   **First fire station:** Ancient Rome in 24 BCE   **Average cost of a new, fully equipped fire engine:** More than £250,000 (US$435,000)

Trucking

Around the clock, trucks of all shapes and sizes freight anything from livestock to flammable substances. Some drivers own their truck, while others drive company-owned vehicles. A driver's job includes keeping detailed log books, loading and unloading cargo, changing heavy tyres, and having a good knowledge of mechanics. Some truck cabins have a small bed for the driver to sleep on after driving long distances.

Overload!

Usually, trucks must comply with strict load limits. However, this truck driver in Somalia, Africa, seems to have ignored any safety rules. The truck is overloaded with harvested corn.

Kings of the road

In the Australian outback, trucks known as road trains lug three or more trailers of goods over long distances between remote towns. The long and heavy multiple trailers make road trains difficult to manoeuvre, and suited only to driving on flat stretches of road that are mostly free of traffic.

Mining giant

Towering at more than 6.7 m (22 ft) tall, massive dump trucks shift hundreds of tonnes of dirt, rocks, and mining materials from quarries and open-pit mines.

Loaded with logs

Log trucks transport felled timber between the forests and sawmills for processing. The timber must be carefully secured to the trailer. Trucks that are used to haul logs are around 30 m (98.4 ft) long.

Trawling tanks

Tankers are trucks with in-built tanks to transport oil, gas, flammable liquids, and other chemicals. Trucks carrying hazardous materials are clearly labelled with their contents in case of an accident or emergency.

Decorative drive

In Pakistan, trucks are ornately painted and carved with designs specific to different regions of the country. Many of these trucks have lucky charms, such as an old shoe, hanging from the bumper bar.

Moving house

In some parts of the USA, you may spot a small house being moved on a truck! Trucks that carry mobile homes must drive very slowly to support their unwieldy load.

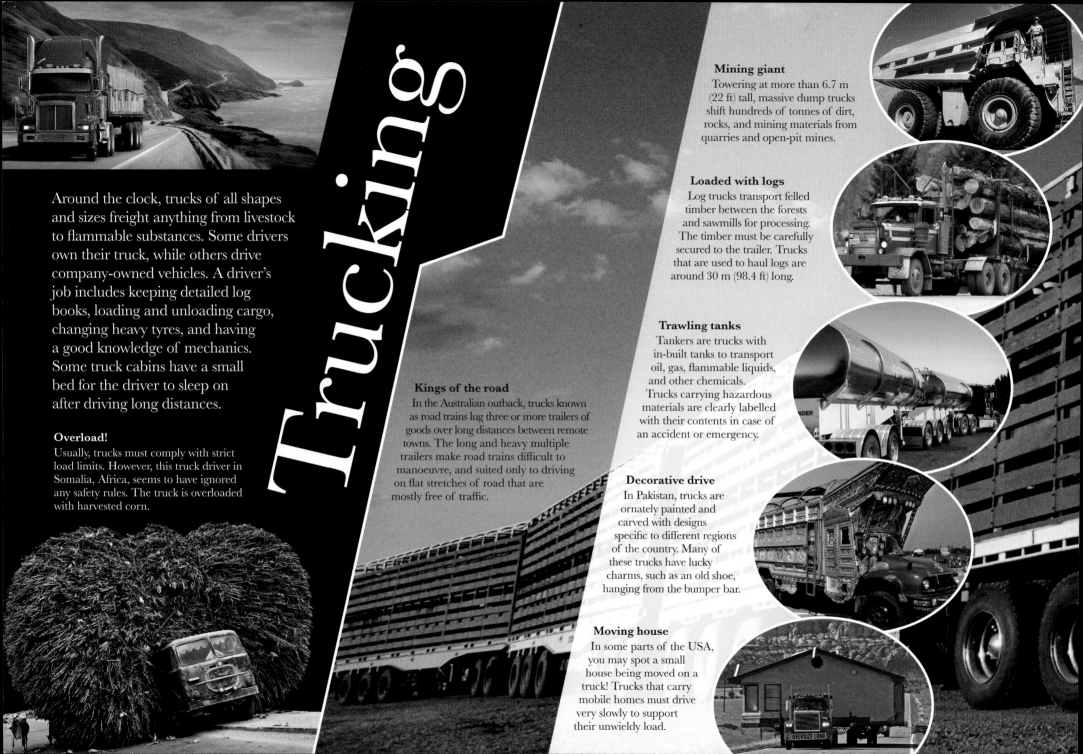

Monster trucks

With names like Grave Digger, Predator, and Avenger, monster trucks are fearsome beasts purpose-built for maximum destruction. To cheering audiences, these terrifying vehicles race around dirt-filled arenas, crushing cars, small planes, and mobile homes with unrelenting force. Monster trucks are supercharged, custom-built vehicles equipped with mammoth 1.7-m (5.6-ft) tyres weighing a hefty 4,082 kg (9,000 lb) or more.

Transformer robot
Transforming from a truck into a 12-m- (39-ft-) tall fire-breathing robotic dinosaur, Robosaurus is an engineering marvel. As it crushes cars in its claws and pulverizes planes in its jaws, Robosaurus mirrors the body movements of its driver, who is connected to high-tech sensors.

Monster racing

Thanks to massive 1,500–2,000 horsepower engines, monster trucks can race short distances at speeds of 161 kph (100 mph). Common events include "side-by-side" racing, where two trucks simultaneously negotiate a track to the finish line, and "freestyle", in which trucks are awarded points for stunts.

Heavy-duty action

Whether they are leaping 7.5 m (25 ft) through the air or performing pogos (bouncing on rear wheels), wheelies (rising on rear wheels), or cyclones (performing high-speed spins), monster trucks need serious suspension. Most monster trucks are fitted with two massive coiled shock absorbers per tyre. Over one year, the punishing work of an average monster truck will have destroyed eight sets of tyres.

Crushing force

The vehicles crushed by monster trucks are usually purchased from scrap yards. Built to destroy virtually any obstacle in their path, monster trucks are fitted with a Remote Ignition Interruptor (RII) emergency switch to stop out-of-control trucks from crossing safety barriers and careering into onlookers.

The original Big Foot

Big Foot is the original monster truck – a souped-up Ford F-250 4x4 pick-up vehicle built to promote an American four-wheel-drive business in the late 1970s. Crushing its first car in 1981, Big Foot has spawned 16 generations of "big feet" and popularized the sport of monster trucking around the world.

Offroad

Navigating offroad terrain demands a specialist vehicle and a particular set of driving skills. For some people, driving offroad is a necessity because they work in areas where the roads are in a poor condition – or even nonexistent. Others go offroad for recreation, enjoying the challenge of trying to get their vehicle up a steep mountainside or across a deep river. Whatever the reason, driving offroad can be a thrilling experience.

Treacherous mud
A major problem of driving in mud is that it is unpredictable. Lowering the tyre pressures can help, especially when driving though sticky mud. It is important that the vehicle stays in one gear and maintains a steady speed to avoid getting stuck.

Offroad trivia

■ Many offroad vehicles incorporate four-wheel drive. This means that power goes to all four wheels rather than just the two front or rear wheels. It gives the vehicle extra control when driving over difficult terrain.

■ Some offroaders have special "low-ratio" gearboxes. Like the smaller cogs on a bicycle, these allow the vehicle to drive up steeper slopes than would be possible to negotiate with a standard gearbox.

■ The best-known offroad cars are British-made Land Rovers and US-made Jeeps. Both were first manufactured more than 60 years ago and have a reputation for strength and durability.

■ Other forms of vehicles that can be hired out at special centres to tackle offroad terrain include trucks, motorbikes, quad bikes, and snowploughs. It is even possible to experience offroad driving in a tank.

Slippery snow

Tyres are the most important consideration when driving on snow and ice. Chunky tyres with deep treads are the best type because they secure the strongest grip. Tyre chains can also be used. Gentle braking is a key driving skill, otherwise the wheels will lock and skid.

Precarious water

Driving through water can be extremely treacherous, especially in potentially deep river crossings. If in any doubt, drivers should avoid crossing a river, otherwise the vehicle could get stuck or even be swept away by strong currents. A low gear is selected before entering the water because changing gear while in it will cause loss of momentum.

Dangerous dunes

Wide tyres are necessary to negotiate massive sand dunes, such as those found in the Namibian desert in Africa. This is because the vehicle has to virtually "float" over the surface of the sand and not sink down into it. Driving in dunes requires very specialist skills and can be dangerous because the vehicle can easily roll over.

Unpredictable savannah

As well as animal hazards such as cheetahs and lions, offroad safari vehicles often encounter terrain that features ridges that were formed, and rocks that were deposited, during the rainy season. Drivers drive slowly to avoid these obstacles.

Dakar Rally

The route of the Dakar is notoriously difficult, and the race is considered an endurance test. Thick mud, dangerous rocks, and sand dunes all feature along the way, pushing drivers to their limits.

When French rally racer Thierry Sabine got lost in the Libyan desert in 1978, he decided that the desolate landscape would be ideal for a rally – a race across rough land and public roads, with rules governing route, time, and speed. The next year, the Dakar Rally was born. This annual rally includes competitive sections known as "Stages" or "Specials". The noncompetitive route to the start of a Special is called a "Liaison".

Motorbike class
The bike category is one of three classes. KTM is the most popular bike, followed by Yamaha. Participants in this category have to look out for uneven ruts made by trucks as these can cause accidents.

Car class
Volkswagen, Mitsubishi, and Nissan are the leaders in the car class, but entries can vary from small trucks to buggies. Frenchman Jean-Louis Schlesser has won the race twice with his custom-made dune buggies.

Truck class
In recent years, Tatra, DAF, Kamaz, and Mercedes-Benz have been the trucks to watch. Some manufacturers use the rally to test the durability of their new trucks, which are often heavily modified to cope with the tough conditions.

Rally route 2005
The route is one of the longest in the world and includes parts of Europe and Africa. Between Barcelona and Dakar, the distances competitors travel vary from a few kilometres to a few hundred kilometres each day. Most of the racers taking part are amateur. In 2005, there were a total of

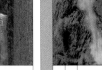

LEG 1 — **31.12.04 Barcelona > Barcelona**
- **Special:** 6 km (4 miles)
- **Liaisons:** 44 km (27 miles)

This was the opening stage of the 2005 Dakar. Known as the Super Special, it established the starting order for the next day. The competitive part took place on the beach.

LEG 2 — **01.01.05 Barcelona > Granada**
- **Noncompetitive leg**
- **Liaison:** 920 km (571 miles)

A ceremony was held in Barcelona to introduce the competitors, who then faced a long, gruelling drive on the motorways to Granada. There was no Special in this leg.

LEG 3 — **02.01.05 Granada > Rabat**
- **Special:** 10 km (6 miles)
- **Liaisons:** 563 km (350 miles)

Before leaving Spain, the racers drove a fast and furious 10-km (6-mile) track on military land near Granada. There was a boat crossing at Algeciras before a smooth run in Africa.

LEG 4 — **03.01.05 Rabat > Agadir**
- **Special:** 123 km (76 miles)
- **Liaisons:** 543 km (337 miles)

This new African Special was littered with traps. Racers passed a cork oak forest, and then the route got difficult as random changes in direction vexed even experienced drivers.

LEG 5 — **04.01.05 Agadir > Smara**
- **Special:** 381 km (237 miles)
- **Liaisons:** 273 km (170 miles)

A warm-up session on a tarmac road to Guelmin prepared the racers for the long Special to follow. High speeds were possible until the terrain became too rocky.

LEG 6 — **05.01.05 Smara > Zouerat**
- **Special:** 660 km (410 miles)
- **Liaison:** 9 km (5.5 miles)

After a long, straight run to the Mauritanian border, the tricky African sand dunes gave the competitors the opportunity to show off their navigational skills.

PORTUGAL

SPAIN

Barcelona ②

Granada ③

LEG 7
06.01.05 Zouerat > Tichit
Special: 660 km (410 miles)
Liaison: 9 km (5.5 miles)

As most of the route was new for 2005, previous experience of the rally did not benefit the racers. This leg included fields and camel grass, as well as a tricky cliff pass.

LEG 8
07.01.05 Tichit > Tidjikja
Special: 520 km (323 miles)
Liaison: 18 km (11 miles)

This was one of the most exciting legs and included stretches from the best Specials of the last 20 years. There were challenging sand dunes to cross on the way to the Nega pass.

LEG 9
08.01.05 Tidjikja > Atar
Special: 361 km (224 miles)
Liaisons: 38 km (24 miles)

This was the final stage before the drivers enjoyed a well-earned rest day. They raced along 300 km (186 miles) of track, before problematic dunes forced them to slow down.

LEG 10
10.01.05 Atar > Atar
Special: 483 km (300 miles)
Liaisons: 16 km (10 miles)

Traditionally, the first stretch after rest day is an easy one. But, in 2005, it was the rally's most difficult sand crossing. The racers travelled on to the Thaga pass.

LEG 11
11.01.05 Atar > Kiffa
Special: 656 km (407 miles)
Liaisons: 39 km (24 miles)

To mark the last day in Mauritania, drivers had to navigate an extended Special of 600 km (373 miles). The first half involved soft dunes, while the second crossed an oasis.

LEG 12
12.01.05 Kiffa > Bamako
Special: 586 km (364 miles)
Liaisons: 233 km (145 miles)

Dense vegetation surrounded this route, making landmarks hard to spot and navigation difficult. Drivers passed through villages and rivers, and even spotted some animals along the way.

LEG 13
13.01.05 Bamako > Kayes
Special: 586 km (364 miles)
Liaisons: 233 km (145 miles)

When the drivers reached this Special, they travelled at top speed because the route was clear. The speed dropped at the Manantali barrage – from here on it was bushland.

LEG 14
14.01.05 Kayes > Tambacounda
Special: 510 km (317 miles)
Liaison: 3 km (2 miles)

The track followed the Senegalese border and narrowed the nearer it got to the Faleme River. This historic spot marks the arrival and finish of the rally in Senegal.

LEG 15
15.01.05 Tambacounda > Dakar
Special: 22 km (14 miles)
Liaisons: 344 km (214 miles)

Competitors travelled a long, tarmac road to the next Special, where the dramatic landscape alternated between tropical forest and rough grassland.

LEG 16
16.01.05 Dakar > Dakar
Special: 31 km (19 miles)
Liaison: 37 km (23 miles)

The outcome of the race was already decided for most competitors. In the Dakar tradition, the final Special was a line-up start on the beach. A prize-giving ceremony ended the rally.

Final check

About 485 vehicles are entered in the Dakar. These all need to be safety-checked to ensure they meet the strict regulations of the event, such as wheel size, speed limit, and the compulsory inclusion of a safety horn.

MOROCCO

WESTERN SAHARA

MAURITANA

MALI

SENEGAL

GUINEA

Agadir 5

Smara 6

Zouerat 7

Atar 10

Tidjikja 9

11

Tichit 8

Kiffa 12

Kayes 14

Tambacounda 15

Bamako 13

Dakar 16

148

青藏铁路工程

Completed in 2006, the Qinghai-Tibet Railway is a miracle of engineering. It reaches across China from Xining, in the northwestern province of Qinghai, to Lhasa, capital of Tibet. It is the first time that Tibet has been linked to the rest of China. Most of the railway's 1,900-km (1,180-mile) length is more than 4,000 m (13,125 ft) above sea level. For five months of the year, temperatures along the route drop to –30°C (–22°F).

Railway in the clouds

Under construction
About 550 km (342 miles) of the rail route crosses permafrost (permanently frozen ground). Workers lowered stretches of track into place on top of the ice.

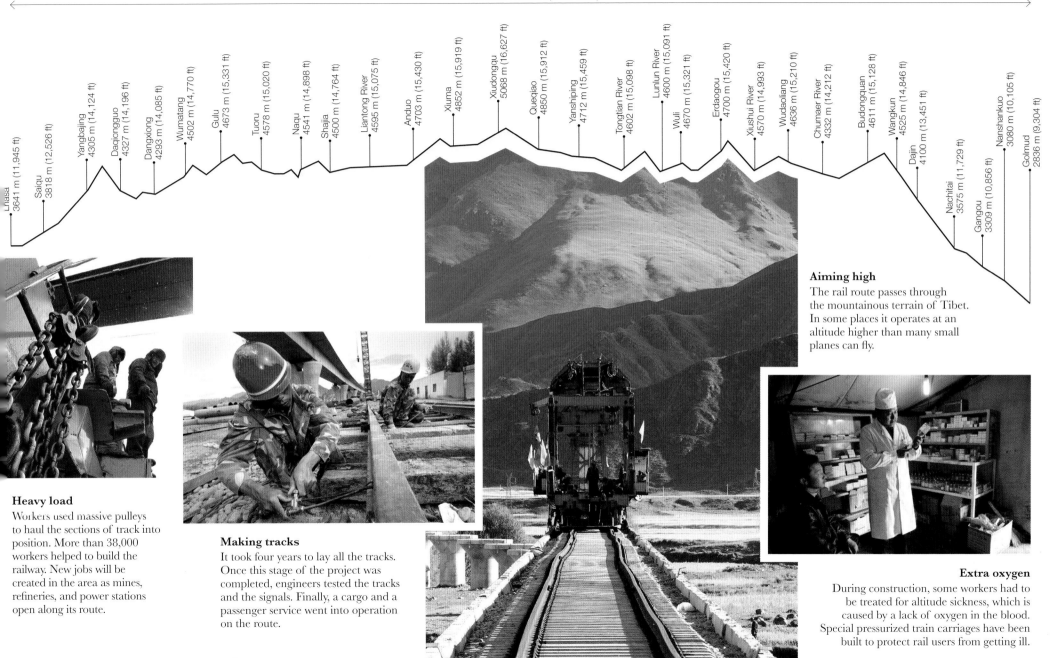

Distance 1,900 km (1,180 miles)

Lhasa 3641 m (11,945 ft)
Saiqu 3818 m (12,526 ft)
Yangbajing 4305 m (14,124 ft)
Daqiongguo 4327 m (14,196 ft)
Dangxiong 4293 m (14,085 ft)
Wumatang 4502 m (14,770 ft)
Gulu 4673 m (15,331 ft)
Tuoru 4578 m (15,020 ft)
Naqu 4541 m (14,898 ft)
Shajia 4500 m (14,764 ft)
Liantong River 4595 m (15,075 ft)
Anduo 4703 m (15,430 ft)
Xiuma 4852 m (15,919 ft)
Xiudongqu 5068 m (16,627 ft)
Queqiao 4850 m (15,912 ft)
Yanshiping 4712 m (15,459 ft)
Tongtian River 4602 m (15,098 ft)
Lunlun River 4600 m (15,091 ft)
Wuli 4670 m (15,321 ft)
Erdaogou 4700 m (15,420 ft)
Xiushui River 4570 m (14,993 ft)
Wudaoliang 4636 m (15,210 ft)
Chumaer River 4332 m (14,212 ft)
Budongquan 4611 m (15,128 ft)
Wangkun 4525 m (14,846 ft)
Dajin 4100 m (13,451 ft)
Nachitai 3575 m (11,729 ft)
Gangou 3309 m (10,856 ft)
Nanshankuo 3080 m (10,105 ft)
Golmud 2836 m (9,304 ft)

Aiming high
The rail route passes through the mountainous terrain of Tibet. In some places it operates at an altitude higher than many small planes can fly.

Heavy load
Workers used massive pulleys to haul the sections of track into position. More than 38,000 workers helped to build the railway. New jobs will be created in the area as mines, refineries, and power stations open along its route.

Making tracks
It took four years to lay all the tracks. Once this stage of the project was completed, engineers tested the tracks and the signals. Finally, a cargo and a passenger service went into operation on the route.

Extra oxygen
During construction, some workers had to be treated for altitude sickness, which is caused by a lack of oxygen in the blood. Special pressurized train carriages have been built to protect rail users from getting ill.

Great rail journeys

All aboard! Some rail journeys are famous for their luxurious trains, while others are celebrated for the awe-inspiring scenery they pass. Whether experienced in an opulent first-class berth or a basic economy-class seat, a great rail journey is a nostalgic return to an old-world style of travel. A train can take days to cross states and continents, rather than a few hours spent on a plane. Chugging through desert, forest, or snow, trains enable passengers to make the most of their journey, by enjoying the landscape and stopping off at locations en route.

The great Siberian
Crossing Russia and travelling into Mongolia and China, the Trans-Siberian Railway is the world's longest railway. The famed 9,288-km (5,772-mile) journey from Moscow to Vladivostok takes seven days, passing through eight time zones.

The opulent Orient Express
Famed for its first-class luxury, the glamorous Venice Simplon-Orient-Express travels through Europe, visiting Istanbul, London, Paris, Prague, Venice, and Vienna.

Camel of the outback
Named after the Afghan camel caravans used to transport early Australian explorers, the Ghan travels 2,979 km (1,851 miles) between Adelaide and Darwin. Riding deep into the outback, the Ghan traverses red, barren desert as it makes its way towards Australia's steamy, tropical north.

Adventure in the Andes
The many wonders of the ancient Incan civilization can be viewed from a single rail trip. PeruRail travels between Cuzco, Lake Titicaca, the Sacred Valley, Arequipa, and the ruins of the ancient citadel, Machu Picchu.

Himalayan steam
India's World Heritage-listed Darjeeling Himalayan railway travels 86 km (53 miles) from Darjeeling to New Jalpaiguri. Steam locomotives have run on the railway since it opened in 1881.

Mountain marvels
In seven-and-a-half hours, Switzerland's Glacier Express connects Zermatt and St. Moritz. The highest peak on the 272-km (169-mile) journey through the Swiss Alps is the Oberalp Pass at 2,033 m (6,670 ft).

South Africa's little gem
Ushering its passengers in five-star comfort through South Africa's famed diamond-mining regions, the Blue Train's regular route is the 1,600-km (994-mile) journey between Pretoria and Cape Town.

Lap of luxury
Travelling through Thailand, Malaysia, and Singapore, the Eastern and Orient Express provides the finest in silver service. On board, the train's cuisine rivals that of the world's best restaurants.

Making tracks

The *Train à Grande Vitesse* (TGV) is a high-speed train that connects many large cities in France. It travels on a specially built network of tracks that enables it to reach speeds of up to 320 kph (199 mph). Variations of the train also operate in the Netherlands, Spain, and the UK, where Eurostar services through the Channel Tunnel use adapted TGVs.

Ventilation slots provide air cooling for the electronic resistors that heat up when the driver slows down the TGV at high speed.

The TGV has four motors in the front power carriage and a further four in the rear carriage, each of which provides power directly to the wheels.

The auxiliary power unit generates the power for the nontraction parts of the TGV, such as carriage lighting and motor cooling fans.

The main transformer converts the electric current from the overhead lines so that it can then be used to drive the power units.

The pantograph obtains electric current from the overhead lines. All TGVs have one at the front of the train and one at the back.

The impact absorption block provides a protective barrier in the event of a collision, though there have been no fatal crashes in the TGV's history.

An automated system in the cab reads signals that are transmitted through sensors in the track, so easing the workload on the driver.

Each of the two power carriages can produce just under 6,000 brake horsepower (a measurement of power) and weighs about 68 tonnes.

At high speeds, the motor gets very hot and is cooled by freon – a gas that is also used in fridges and air-conditioning systems.

The frame upon which the motors are positioned is made of high-grade steel that is both light and strong.

Each carriage has two pairs of wheels at the front and two at the rear. The thrust is transmitted through the wheels in the two power carriages.

The suspension system is made up of primary and secondary springs, though more recent TGVs use air-filled suspension units.

Every carriage incorporates a large luggage compartment, and some TGVs allow bicycles to be transported.

TGVs on each line have different carriage arrangements – the TGV Atlantique is made up of two power carriages and ten passenger carriages.

The TGV can operate in other countries where the power current in the overhead cables is different to that found in France.

A typical ten-carriage TGV Atlantique will include 13 toilets, plus separate baby-changing facilities.

In 1990, a shortened TGV Atlantique set a world record speed for a conventional train of 515 kph (320 mph).

The frames upon which the axle, wheels, suspension, gearing, and brake components are mounted are called bogies.

On the TGV Atlantique, there are three first-class carriages, which are usually located at the front of the train.

The TGV Atlantique can seat 465 passengers, but the double-decker TGV Duplex is able to accommodate up to 1,024 people.

The high-tech nature of the train and track means that passengers sitting in a TGV carriage experience a vibration-free, quiet journey.

While the TGV is designed to run on specially constructed high-speed track, it can also operate on normal lines, but at lower speeds.

The commuters

A constant stream of commuters pours through Grand Central Terminal 24 hours a day. Arriving on Metro-North Railroad trains from towns north of New York City, many passengers continue their journeys from the terminal's busy subway station.

Jeremy and Michael

Jeremy loves trains and enjoys visiting Grand Central Terminal with his father, Michael. "In New York, subways are a part of life," says Michael. "We take the subway to go shopping, visit our friends, or go on exciting adventures!"

Tolga and Oliver

Tolga and Oliver are British actors visiting New York for a film premiere. "We bought one-day passes for $7 (£4). The subway makes it easy to travel all over the city."

Jitendra and Gurmeet

"There is a lot of history behind Grand Central. It's a unique place, and it's very efficient, too – I cannot remember having to wait too long for the trains. It's well organized."

Isao and friends

"We are coffee shop managers from Tokyo visiting New York City on a business trip. Later, we will take the subway to West 60th Street. Now we are eating crêpes and drinking coffee!"

Michael

"When I'm in the New York area, I often take trains to Boston and Washington, DC. I much prefer trains to planes as it's a more comfortable and easy-going journey."

Lining the platform

Grand Central Terminal has 44 platforms where suburban and long-distance trains stop between 5.30 am and 1.30 am every day. Spanning two levels, the platforms service 67 tracks – 41 are on the top level and 26 are on the lower level.

Terminal trivia

- Grand Central Terminal stretches across 0.2 sq km (49 acres) and is one of the world's largest train stations.
- 125,000 people commute through the terminal each day.

- 570,000 people visit the terminal each day to shop, sightsee, or eat in the restaurants and cafés.
- Ninety-eight per cent of trains arrive at Grand Central Terminal on schedule.

- More than 660 Metro-North trains serve the terminal daily, while trains pass through the terminal's subway station every few minutes.
- There are 25 automated ticket vending machines located throughout the terminal.

- 30,000 bulbs are used to light Grand Central Terminal each year.
- More than five tonnes of newspapers are collected throughout the terminal for recycling every day.

Famed for its architecture, Grand Central Terminal in New York City is both an icon for the city and a symbol of the railways. It is a bustling transport hub, with more than half a million people passing through each day. Trains arrive from and depart to towns in New York State and Connecticut, and the subway station is the city's busiest.

Grand Central Terminal
New York City

Walking the marble floor
Filled with commuters and visitors moving in every direction, the terminal's main concourse is 61 m (200 ft) long. Light pours into the terminal through the three 18-m- (60-ft-) high arched windows.

The workers

Grand Central Terminal provides jobs for more than one thousand people. Some work on the trains as engineers and conductors, or help customers at the information desks. Others are employed in the terminal's shops and restaurants.

Luis

Luis is a police officer patrolling the terminal. "I make sure that everything is safe, secure, and running smoothly. Every day is different. Some days I help sick or injured people, but mostly I answer people's questions."

Pat

"I inspect tickets, answer questions, and ensure passengers get on and off the train safely. I also help decide how many carriages we need on the train," explains Pat, a conductor on the New Haven line.

Tom

Tom is the automated ticket sales manager at the terminal. "There are around 7,000 tickets in each vending machine. Most ticket machines are restocked every two or three weeks."

Bill

As a locomotive simulator technician, Bill operates computers that new engineers use to practise driving trains. "It's important that student engineers are familiar with the cab and using the controls before driving a real train."

Mike

Mike works in the terminal's very busy lost property office, which recovers 19,000 items each year. "A strange time was when we had three people looking for two sets of false teeth. One guy wanted to try them all out!"

Audrey

In the Centre Information Booth, customer services manager Audrey is asked up to 1,000 questions an hour. "We can refer to computers and information boards, but the answers soon become second nature!"

Keeping on track

- Established in 1913, the Oyster Bar serves more than 20,000 oysters every day.
- Proposing marriage in the Whispering Gallery next to the Oyster Bar is a New York City tradition.

- More than 10,000 meals are served in the terminal's cafes and restaurants each day.
- A master clock synchronizes all of the terminal's clocks to ensure accuracy up to one-billionth of a second.

- 60 rail traffic controllers direct trains on the lines that enter and leave the terminal.
- 100 conductors stamp tickets, collect fares, and assist passengers to safely board and exit Metro-North trains.

- 50 cleaners work shifts throughout the extensive terminal.
- Transit Bureau, a division of the New York Police Department, patrols Grand Central Terminal and the greater rail network.

0 — 60

Start your engines! With pedals to the metal, motor races are charged with high-octane atmosphere. Tyres squeal and rubber burns in the quest for the chequered flag. In the United States, NASCAR, IndyCar, and top-fuel drag racing reign supreme, while in Europe and much of Asia, the number one motorsport championships are the Formula One Grand Prix and MotoGP grand prix series.

Formula One (F1) Grand Prix
F1 is the top class of motor racing, and the world's most expensive sport. Race teams compete for the Drivers' and Constructors' World Championships each year. Since 1984, the Ferrari, McLaren, Renault, and Williams teams have dominated the F1 championships.

NASCAR (National Association for Stock Car Auto Racing)
Exceeding 321 kph (200 mph), NASCARs are high-powered racing cars fitted with thin sheet-metal bodies to look like stock (road) cars. In North America, dozens of tracks host more than 100 races each year. The largest NASCAR competitions are the Nextel Cup, the Busch Series, and the Craftsman Truck Series.

Motorcycle Grand Prix (MotoGP)
With an annual series of 17 rounds in 15 countries, each Motorcycle Grand Prix race lasts just 45 minutes without pitstops. Powered by 990 cc four-stroke engines, MotoGP bikes have technology unavailable on road-going motorcycles.

IndyCar
Fitted with methanol engines, IndyCars produce more than 650 horsepower, going from 0–96.5 kph (0–60 mph) in less than three seconds. The most famous IndyCar event is the Indianapolis 500, where drivers cover 200 laps of the 4.02-km (2.5-mile) circuit, equalling 804.6 km (500 miles).

McLaren F1
Launched in 1993, the super-exotic McLaren F1 is one of the fastest cars to go on sale to the public. With only 100 cars manufactured, the McLaren F1 is also one of the most expensive road cars, costing around £630,000 (US$1,105,765). Equipped with a 6.1-litre V12 BMW engine, the McLaren F1's maximum speed is 386.4 kph (240 mph).

Rallycross
Audiences lining the safety barriers at a rallycross event eagerly await excitement-packed racing. In Rallycross, rivals race each other across tarmac roads and muddy tracks. Rallycross cars look like their regular road counterparts, such the Ford Fiesta or Focus, yet they are purpose-built, hi-tech racing monsters!

Top-fuel drag racing
Soaring along a 400-m (0.25-mile) strip in less than 4.5 seconds, a top-fuel dragster is powered by 85 per cent nitromethane and 15 per cent methanol (racing alcohol). Rocketing to 450 kph (280 mph) in just 200 m (656 ft), dragsters are equipped with parachutes to help them slow down. Before a run, drivers must warm their tyres by spinning them in a spectacular "burn out".

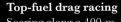

Front forks provide suspension as they move by up to 30 cm (11.5 in) to absorb impact.

The front mudguard prevents mud thrown up from the wheel obscuring the rider's view.

Stunt show

It's show time and you've got a front-row seat! This action-packed motorcycle show stars ex-world championship motocross rider Jason Smyth. Motocross involves motorcycle racing over tough, cross-country terrain, and this is where the stuntman learnt his tricks. He now performs a range of heart-stopping feats at locations around Europe, adapting his display to the size of each venue. In small 50 m (164 ft) by 20 m (66 ft) arenas, mini-bikes are ridden, while at larger sites more powerful 250 cc machines can be used.

Shin guards, knee
braces, and padded
trousers protect the
lower half of the body.

Silencer at the end of the
exhaust pipe muffles
the engine noise.

Breather and overflow
pipes prevent the engine
flooding during stunts.

Soft, strong tyres provide
maximum grip when
landing on ramps.

Motocross cycles

Today, the most popular form
of amateur motorcycle racing
is motocross. The bikes are
lightweight and geared for rapid
acceleration rather than continual top
speeds. Due to the number of tricky
landings, the suspension system is highly
absorbent, and a long saddle covers the
fuel tank to protect the rider.

Catching the rings

This stunt relies on accurate judgement of distance.
The stuntman builds up a speed of 64 kph (40 mph), before
mounting a starting ramp and taking off. The distance between
the starting ramp and the landing ramp is about 25 m (82 ft).
Between the ramps is a pole with rings attached to it. The stuntman
catches these rings 9 m (30 ft) up in the air before landing hands-free
on a ramp, which is covered in mesh to maximize grip.

Stand-up wheelie

The stuntman crashes most often during
ground stunts. The KTM SX 250 bike
is used because it has soft suspension
and hand guards. Speeds of up to 80 kph
(50 mph) are reached during wheelies.

One-handed stoppie

When the stuntman rides only on the
front wheel, it is called a "stoppie".
Regularly performing stoppies causes
huge pressure on the wheels. They buckle
under the strain and have to be replaced.

Cool rides

From thrilling rides on open country roads to winding in and out of jammed peak-hour traffic, motorcycles provide riders with a cheaper, cooler, and less cumbersome alternative to driving a car. While motorcycles are often used as a means of everyday transport, there are also many that take pride of place in their owner's garage, reserved for special rides on the weekends and holidays. Serious motorcycle enthusiasts choose their bikes based on their high performance, fine styling, and collectability. Whether it is a classic Norton, Ducati, Triumph, or Harley-Davidson, for some collectors money is no object when it comes to buying their dream machine.

BAT, 1904
Top speed: 40 kph (25 mph)
Power: 500 cc
Country of origin: UK

Indian 1914 V-Twin, 1914
Top speed: 89 kph (55 mph)
Power: 1,000 cc
Country of origin: USA

Ace, 1919
Top speed: 105 kph (65 mph)
Power: 1,229 cc
Country of origin: USA

Megola Racing Model, 1923
Top speed: 109 kph (69 mph)
Power: 640 cc
Country of origin: Germany

Temple-Anzani, 1923
Top speed: 195 kph (121 mph)
Power: 116 cc
Country of origin: UK

Böhmerland, 1927
Top speed: 95 kph (59 mph)
Power: 603 cc
Country of origin: Czech Republic

Ariel Square-Four, 1931
Top speed: 137 kph (85 mph)
Power: 597 cc
Country of origin: UK

BMW Kompressor, 1935
Top speed: 210 kph (130 mph)
Power: 492 cc
Country of origin: Germany

Indian Sports Scout, 1937
Top speed: 169 kph (105 mph)
Power: 745 cc
Country of origin: USA

Norton 500, 1938
Top speed: 177 kph (110 mph)
Power: 490 cc
Country of origin: UK

Brough Superior Dream, 1938
Top speed: Not known
Power: 998 cc
Country of origin: UK

**Vincent-HRD
Series C Black Shadow, 1949**
Top speed: 196 kph (122 mph)
Power: 998 cc
Country of origin: UK

Zündapp KS601, 1950
Top speed: 140 kph (87 mph)
Power: 597 cc
Country of origin: Germany

Indian Chief Roadmaster, 1950
Top speed: 137 kph (85 mph)
Power: 1,311 cc
Country of origin: USA

Victoria Bergmeister, 1954
Top speed: 130 kph (81 mph)
Power: 347 cc
Country of origin: Germany

Matchless G45, 1957
Top speed: 193 kph (120 mph)
Power: 498 cc
Country of origin: UK

Gritzner Monza Super Sport, 1960
Top speed: 60 kph (37 mph)
Power: 50 cc
Country of origin: Germany

Norton 650SS Dominator, 1962
Top speed: 185 kph (115 mph)
Power: 646 cc
Country of origin: UK

Yamaha YDS3C Big Bear, 1965
Top speed: 142 kph (88 mph)
Power: 246 cc
Country of origin: Japan

BSA Rocket 3, 1969
Top speed: 196 kph (122 mph)
Power: 740 cc
Country of origin: UK

Triumph Trident Racer, 1971
Top speed: 264 kph (164 mph)
Power: 749 cc
Country of origin: UK

Suzuki GT750, 1971
Top speed: 174 kph (108 mph)
Power: 738 cc
Country of origin: Japan

Honda Goldwing GL1500, 1975
Top speed: 187 kph (116 mph)
Power: 1,520 cc
Country of origin: Japan

Fantic Chopper, 1977
Top speed: 105 kph (65 mph)
Power: 123 cc
Country of origin: Italy

Yamaha TZ250, 1979
Top speed: 225 kph (140 mph)
Power: 247 cc
Country of origin: Japan

Laverda Jota, 1982
Top speed: 224 kph (139 mph)
Power: 980 cc
Country of origin: Italy

BMW K1, 1983
Top speed: 201 kph (125 mph)
Power: 988 cc
Country of origin: Germany

Harley-Davidson FLHX Electra Glide, 1984
Top speed: 145 kph (90 mph)
Power: 1,312 cc
Country of origin: USA

Aprilia RSV250, 1990
Top speed: 250 kph (155 mph)
Power: 249 cc
Country of origin: Italy

Kawasaki ZZ-R1100, 1990
Top speed: 282 kph (175 mph)
Power: 1,052 cc
Country of origin: Japan

Honda XRV750, 1991
Top speed: 185 kph (115 mph)
Power: 742 cc
Country of origin: Japan

Husqvarna TC610, 1992
Top speed: 145 kph (90 mph)
Power: 577 cc
Country of origin: Sweden

Ducati M900 Monster, 1994
Top speed: 192 kph (119 mph)
Power: 904 cc
Country of origin: Italy

Suzuki GSX1300R Hayabusa, 1999
Top speed: 299 kph (186 mph)
Power: 1,299 cc
Country of origin: Japan

Yamaha YZF1000 R1, 2001
Top speed: 266 kph (165 mph)
Power: 998 cc
Country of origin: Japan

Harley-Davidson VRSCA V-ROD, 2003
Top speed: 225 kph (140 mph)
Power: 1,130 cc
Country of origin: USA

Legendary chopper
The Harley-Davidson Chopper was immortalized in the 1969 road movie *Easy Rider*, which followed the adventures of two drop-out bikers. The Chopper's unique styling has very high handlebars and two different-sized wheels.

Easy rider

Harley-Davidson motorbikes, affectionately known as "Harleys" or "hogs", are big, heavy, and intended for long-distance, laid-back cruising. More than any other bikes, they are associated with alternative lifestyles and symbolize the freedom of the open road. Harleys look the part with classy chrome styling, and they sound it, too – their engines, usually air-cooled, produce a distinctive, deep rumble.

Feeling sporty
The Harley-Davidson Sportster has been in production since 1957 – longer than any other Harley. Sportsters are the lightest and raciest Harley-Davidson bikes. The 1200 Sportster's top speed is 177 kph (110 mph).

Need for speed
Staged on a straight, flat 400-m (0.25 mile) course, drag-racing events are all about reaching maximum speeds. The "trailer" on the back of the drag bike is a set of wheelie bars that prevent the front wheel lifting too far off the ground when the bike is accelerating.

Born to be wild

Harley owners are passionate about their bikes and love to ride them in big groups. This rally took place outside Moscow, but the world's largest motorcycle event is the Harley-Davidson Love Ride rally, held in California each November. An association for Harley owners, the Harley Owners Group (HOG), was founded in 1983.

Sidecar action

A bike and a passenger sidecar are known as an "outfit". Harley-Davidson started making sidecars in 1914. In the 1920s, the company sold one sidecar for every two bikes. Harley-Davidson's Classic sidecar was produced between 1937 and 1966.

Law enforcement

Harley-Davidson sold its first police bike in 1908. The Harley's speed and manoeuvrability make it especially suitable for use by traffic police, but other law enforcers ride them, too. Today, more than 3,000 police departments across the USA use Harley-Davidsons.

HARLEY-DAVIDSON

William S Harley and Arthur Davidson of Milwaukee, Wisconsin, USA, sold their first motorcycle in 1903. By 1920, the Harley-Davidson Motor Company was the world's largest manufacturer of motorcycles. The famous bar-and-shield logo was patented as early as 1910, and the distinctive eagle design was added in 1933. Harley-Davidson motorcycles have been recognizable everywhere for their fine styling ever since.

Oldest	405 cc Single, debuted in 1903
Fastest	1994 VR1000, reaches top speeds of 306 kph (190 mph)
Heaviest	1989 FLTC Tour-Glide, weighs a hefty 332kg (732 lbs)

VRSCA V-Rod

Launched in 2001, the VRSCA V-Rod was the most radically different Harley model in 50 years. Its liquid-cooled engine is extremely powerful (capable of 115 hp), and can take the bike to a top speed of 225 kph (140 mph).

1903 HARLEY-DAVIDSON 2003

Speedometer

Dummy fuel tank

Engine

Tubular frame

Forks

Alloy wheel

Chrome silencer

Gearbox

Cooling radiator

Speedway

Racing motorbikes on oval dirt tracks first became popular in the 1920s. Speedway bikes are small and light, and they have no brakes, rear suspension, or gears. The races are usually between four riders, who score points depending on their performance over a set number of laps – three points for first place, two for second, one for third, and none for coming last. At the end of the heats, the rider with the most points is the champion. The biggest international tournament is the Fédération Internationale de Motorcyclisme (FIM) Speedway Grand Prix series.

Powersliding

Speedway tracks are covered in a sandy grit called shale. Although the bikes cannot brake as they enter a bend, the loose shale allows them to slide sideways – a technique known as powersliding. During the slide, the bike loses some speed through the back wheel, but keeps enough power to drive on around the bend.

Speedway facts

- A speedway track must be between 260 m (855 ft) and 425 m (1,395 ft) long.

- Longtrack is similar to speedway, but takes place on a 1,000-m (3,280-ft) track and is much faster.

- Many speedway riders learn their skills on grasstrack racing, where they ride larger bikes on grass rather than shale circuits.

- The first ever speedway races took place in Australia in 1923. They were organized by New Zealander Johnny Hoskins.

- A klaxon hooter or a bell sounds a two-minute warning before each heat, so that the riders can prepare to race.

- The heat winner is the rider whose front wheel passes over the finish line first, after completing all the laps (usually four).

Around the circuit
The countries where speedway is most popular are Poland, Sweden, Denmark, and the UK. Speedway meetings attract large crowds. A speedway meeting may have more than 20 heats, but each heat is over in less than a minute.

Speedway sidecar racing

Ordinary sidecars are attached to the side of a motorbike to carry a passenger. Sidecars built for speedway are an integral part of the machine. The sidecars are low to the ground and whip up tremendous plumes of dust as they zoom around the dirt track.

Ice racing

One of the strangest kinds of motorcycle racing is ice racing. The riders speed their brakeless bikes around an ice-covered stadium track. They accelerate to 130 kph (81 mph) on the straights, lean through the turns, and angle for the inside position. Ice racing began in Germany in 1925. The earliest races took place on frozen lakes.

Throttle

Fuel tank

Front suspension damper

Mudguard

Rear-wheel disc

Rear-wheel dirt deflector

Single cylinder four-stroke engine

The front tyre has a maximum width of 100 mm (4 in).

Serious spikes

For better traction on the frozen track, ice-racing bike tyres are studded with hundreds of screws or spikes, some as long as 6.5 cm (2.5 in). The bikes have two-speed gearboxes, too. Riders still take plenty of tumbles, so they wear safety helmets and thick, padded leather suits to protect themselves.

Built for speed

A speedway bike has about the same accelerating power as a Formula One racing car. It has a 500 cc single-cylinder four-stroke engine that runs on pure methanol (racing alcohol), rather than petrol, for safety reasons – methanol is less likely to explode in the event of a crash.

Road racer

The sporty Multistrada 1000S DS motorcycle is produced by Italian motorbike manufacturer, Ducati. The bike's name, "Multistrada", means "many road", and it is designed to be ridden on all types of road surface, from city streets to motorways. The result is a bike that is fast and nimble but is still comfortable. There is even an extra seat so a passenger can hop on, hold on to the grab rail, and experience the thrilling ride!

Racing red
The colour of Ducati's bikes is limited to a small palette. This Multistrada also comes in black, and some models are available in yellow, but Ducati red remains the manufacturer's most famous colour. Why red? In the early days of international racing, red was the colour chosen by Italian competitors, just as "racing green" was the choice of the English entrants.

Comfort and safety
The single rear shock absorber is adjustable, which allows the handling to be altered to suit different riders. The drilled brake discs at the centre of the wheels help to improve braking consistency. In wet weather, the drill-holes prevent a film of water from forming over the discs.

DUCATI

1000 S DS

Front view

Rear view

Stand

Light switch and cable

Rear shock absorber

Clutch lever

Tie rod for suspension

Rear sprocket

Clip, nut, and washer

Rear exhaust

Head protection
Early helmets were made of soft materials that simply cushioned the rider's head. Modern helmets incorporate layered materials, including plastic, so they provide more effective protection.

Safety gear
The correct clothing is essential for a motorcyclist's safety. As bikes have become faster, specialist body armour made mainly from leather has been developed. The leather is treated to ensure suppleness and absorb impact.

Performance rubber
The engine's power goes to the rear wheel, and the extra width of the rear tyre provides added stability. Both front and rear tyres are grooved for use on the road. They are made from a "sticky" rubber that enables them to grip on the road surface.

DUCATI

Multistrada 1000S

Biggest bus fleet
The Andhra Pradesh State Road Transport Company in southern India runs more than 18,300 buses.

Most popular car
Toyota Corollas were first produced in 1966. Since then, more than 25 million Toyota Corollas have been made worldwide.

High rollers
The world's longest convoy of Rolls-Royces was on 20 May 2000, when 420 cars drove for 3.2 km (2 miles) along the A55 near Chester, UK.

Longest train ride
The world's longest single train ride is on the Trans-Siberian Railway. The journey takes eight days and crosses 10,214 km (6,346 miles) from Moscow, Russia, to Pyongyang, North Korea.

Most subway stops
The MTA subway system in New York City has the most subway stops, with 468 stations in a network of 370 km (230 miles).

Longest limousine
The world's longest car is a 30.5-m (100-ft) limousine built in California, USA. It has six wheels, a swimming pool, and a king-size waterbed.

Fastest cyclist
The fastest bicycle speed is 268.8 kph (167 mph), achieved by Dutchman Fred Rompelberg at Bonneville Salt Flats, Utah, USA, on 3 October 1995.

Land records

As people strive for land transport to be bigger, better, more powerful, and more efficient, the record books are bursting with land-lubbing firsts. New records are made and old records are broken, from the busiest railways to the longest motorcycle journeys. There are also marvels of engineering, including the construction of a freight train that was 682 carriages long; and the most outlandish of stretch limousines that has its own swimming pool!

Longest freight train
The record for the largest freight train is 7.4 km (4.6 miles) long. It consisted of 682 carriages and was assembled by Australia's BHP mining company in 2001.

Best-selling vehicle
Since 1958, the Honda Motor Company sold more than 50 million Honda Super Cub motorcycles, making it the most popular vehicle ever.

Most people to fit in a Mini
On 3 July 2000, a record-breaking 18 people crammed into a Mini Cooper car in Birmingham, UK.

Longest journey on a motorbike
Between January 1985 and April 1995, Emilio Scotto of Argentina rode the world's longest motorcycle journey, crossing 214 countries, and (457,000 miles) 735,000 km

Highest monster truck jump
'Bigfoot' made the world's highest monster truck jump, soaring 7.3 metres (24 ft) in Las Vegas, USA, on 14 December 1999.

Longest road train
On 18 February 2006, the world's longest road train hauled 113 trailers and measured 1,474.3 m (4,836.9 ft) on its short 150 m (490 ft) journey in Queensland, Australia.

Busiest railway
The East Japan Railway Company is the world's busiest railway. Every day, the railway carries around 16 million passengers in the eastern parts of Japan, including the city of Tokyo.

Air

Timeline

MODEL OF A DA VINCI FLYING MACHINE

Flying machine
Italian artist Leonardo da Vinci studies the motion of birds in flight and produces a number of drawings of human-powered flight. He also makes sketches of a helicopter-like flying machine.

DRAWING OF GIFFARD'S AIRSHIP

Propelled airship
Frenchman Henri Giffard creates the first powered airship. The hydrogen-filled structure, propelled by a steam engine, travels for 27 km (16.8 miles).

ARTWORK OF *WRIGHT FLYER*

Powered flight
Bicycle engineers Wilbur and Orville Wright develop the *Wright Flyer*, which becomes the first piloted, powered aircraft to achieve sustained flight. They go on to set up their own aircraft company.

MODEL OF *BLERIOT XI*

Cross-Channel hero
French inventor Louis Bleriot is the first person to fly across the English Channel. He makes the 37-minute flight in a plane he designed himself, the *Bleriot XI*.

DOUGLAS WORLD CRUISER

Global trip
Two specially built aircraft – the Douglas World Cruisers – become the first planes to circumnavigate the Earth. The journey takes six months and covers almost 40,572 km (25,195 miles).

c. 1500   1852   1903   1909   1924

1783   1853   1907   1919   1927

Hot-air balloon
French brothers Joseph and Etienne Montgolfier carry out experiments with hot-air balloons. After sending a sheep, a chicken, and a duck up in a balloon, a later version becomes the first hot-air balloon to lift humans into the air, rising up 90 m (295 ft) and travelling for 10 km (6.2 miles).

PAINTING OF MONTGOLFIER BROTHERS' BALLOON

Glider pioneer
Regarded as a true pioneer of the principles of flight, Englishman George Cayley develops a series of primitive gliding machines that culminates in the first glider to lift an adult into the air.

DRAWING OF CAYLEY'S GLIDER

Rotor flight
The first person to achieve vertical flight in a powered craft is Frenchman Paul Cornu. His primitive "helicopter" only just rises into the air, but manages to stay aloft for 20 seconds.

CORNU'S ROTOR CRAFT

Atlantic endeavours
Englishmen John Alcock and Arthur Whitten-Brown complete an epic 16-hour flight across the Atlantic Ocean in a Vickers Vimy. Battling through snow and fog, they become the first pilots to make the journey nonstop.

ALCOCK AND WHITTEN-BROWN'S VIMY

Solo flight
In his *Spirit of St Louis* aircraft, US pilot Charles Lindbergh becomes the first person to fly solo across the Atlantic Ocean. An enthusiastic crowd of more than 100,000 people awaits him as he lands in France.

DRAWING OF *SPIRIT OF ST LOUIS*

Jet-powered flight
The German Heinkel He 178, the world's first jet-powered aircraft, makes its maiden flight. It has short wooden wings and can fly at speeds in excess of 644 kph (400 mph).

Passenger airliner
The De Havilland DH106 Comet takes off for the first time. It is designed to be the world's first commercial jet airliner, and becomes fully operational after three more years of testing. It can carry more passengers faster around the world than any previous aircraft.

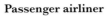

Supersonic flight
The prototype of the Russian Tupolev Tu-144 takes to the skies. It becomes the first commercial airliner to travel at Mach 2 (twice the speed of sound).

Atlantic crossing
Piloted by Ben Abruzzo, Maxie Anderson, and Larry Newman, *Double Eagle II* becomes the first balloon to fly across the Atlantic Ocean. After setting off from Maine, USA, the balloon lands in a field north of Paris, France, almost six days later.

Balloon adventure
Bertrand Piccard from Switzerland and Briton Brian Jones complete the first circumnavigation of the world in a balloon. Their *Breitling Orbiter 3* takes just under 20 days to make the trip.

1939 1947 1949 1961 1968 1969 1978 1981 1999 2005

Breaking the sound barrier
US test pilot Charles "Chuck" Yeager becomes the fastest man on Earth when his Bell X-1 rocket-powered aircraft exceeds the speed of sound while flying at 13,110 m (43,027 ft) over the Mojave Desert in California, USA.

Human in space
Russian cosmonaut Yuri Gagarin is the first person to orbit Earth. At the end of his 108-minute flight in *Vostok I*, he ejects from the craft and parachutes safely down to Earth.

Moon landing
American Neil Armstrong lands the *Eagle* lunar module on the Moon. Armstrong and fellow astronaut Buzz Aldrin become the first people to walk on the surface of the Moon.

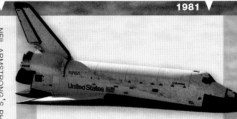

Reusable spacecraft
Exactly 20 years to the day after Yuri Gagarin's debut space flight, the world's first reusable spacecraft, the Space Shuttle *Columbia*, embarks on its maiden mission. After orbiting Earth for about 55 hours, *Columbia* lands on a runway in California, USA.

Mammoth aircraft
The world's biggest passenger airliner, the Airbus A380, makes its maiden flight from Toulouse, France. Once operational, it will be able to carry more than 850 passengers.

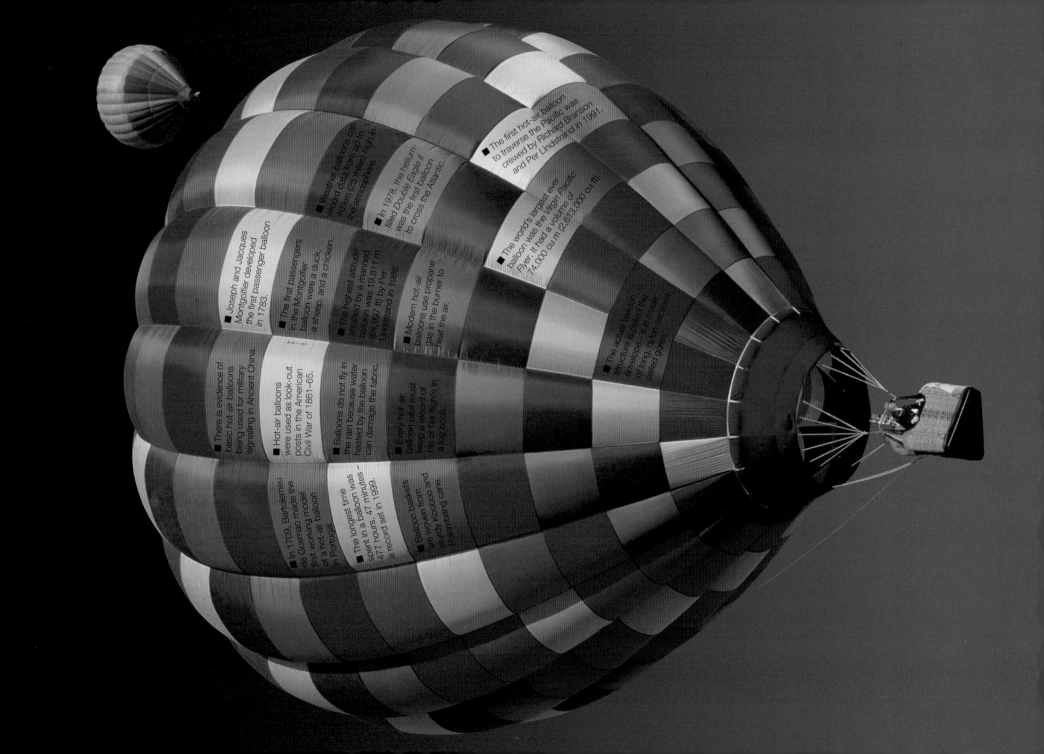

- The first hot-air balloon to traverse the Pacific was crewed by Richard Branson and Per Lindstrand in 1991.

- The world's largest ever balloon was the Virgin Pacific Flyer. It had a volume of 74,000 cu m (2,613,000 cu ft).

- The actual balloon structure is called the envelope. It is made of long, triangular sections called gores.

- Weather balloons can record data from up to 40 km (25 miles) high in the atmosphere.

- In 1978, the helium-filled Double Eagle II was the first balloon to cross the Atlantic.

- Modern hot-air balloons use propane gas in the burner to heat the air.

- Joseph and Jacques Montgolfier developed the first passenger balloon in 1783.

- The first passengers in the Montgolfier balloon were a duck, a sheep, and a chicken.

- The highest altitude attained by a manned balloon was 19,811 m (64,997 ft) by Per Lindstrand in 1988.

- There is evidence of basic hot-air balloons being used for military signalling in Ancient China.

- Hot-air balloons were used as look-out posts in the American Civil War of 1861–65.

- Balloons do not fly in the rain because water heated by the balloon can damage the fabric.

- Every hot-air balloon pilot must keep a record of his or her flights in a log book.

- In 1709, Bartolemeu de Gusmao made the first working model of a hot air balloon in Portugal.

- The longest time spent in a balloon was 477 hours, 47 minutes – a record set in 1999.

- Balloon baskets are woven from sturdy Kooboo and Palembang cane.

Hot air

The oldest human flight technology, hot-air balloons can be made into almost any shape, although the upside-down teardrop is the most common. Passengers are carried in a lightweight wicker basket. Liquid gas in cylinders positioned at the base of the balloon heats the air in the balloon, and this makes it rise up. The balloonist manoeuvres the balloon by climbing to different wind currents at different altitudes. When it is time to descend, hot air is slowly released.

- An airship differs from a balloon in that it can be propelled through the air.

- The bottom part of the envelope is called the skirt and is made of a flame-resistant material.

- For most nylon envelopes the maximum internal temperature is limited to about 120°C (248°F).

- Balloon pilots need a specialist balloon pilot's licence to fly a balloon.

- The biggest hot-air balloons are able to carry 20 passengers.

- Before it is fully inflated, a balloon is often attached to a vehicle—or to the ground.

- The fastest circumnavigation of the world in a balloon was 320 hours and 33 minutes by Spirit of Freedom in 2002.

- Hot-air balloons are almost silent, so they are an ideal way of observing wildlife on a safari.

- The largest in the world is the annual Albuquerque International Balloon Fiesta, where up to 730 balloons are flown.

- The world's largest balloon manufacturers are based in England. Cameron builds about 500 balloons a year.

- Pre-flight, pilots sometimes release a helium-filled balloon to check the wind direction.

- A hot-air balloon pilot travels by flying with air currents.

- A ground crew follows a balloon and picks up its passengers when it lands.

- Instruments on board a hot-air balloon measure the balloon's speed, altitude, and the rate at which it is rising or falling.

- In 1999, the Breitling Orbiter 3 made the first successful round-the-world trip in a balloon.

Airships

Zeppelin NT
A modern version of the legendary German Zeppelin company has developed an airship called the NT ("New Technology"). Designed for advertising and research purposes, it first flew in September 1997.

While the airships of today are more advanced than those that flew in the "golden age" of airships in the 1920s and 1930s, the principles of this type of flight remain exactly the same. Essentially, a container holds a gas that is lighter than the air outside of it, thereby raising it into the sky. This can be achieved either by inserting the gas – usually helium – into a framework covered with fabric, or simply by filling the material with gas and expanding it.

Futuristic design
This Canadian airship has been created using the latest technology. Its unique spherical design – it is shaped like a football – has no stabilizing fins, and the crew actually sit within the structure rather than in an external cabin. In 2003, it set a manned airship altitude world record when it flew up to 6,234 m (20,460 ft). An attempt at a round-the-world flight is planned for the future.

Blimps
Non-rigid airships have no frame inside them and are commonly known as blimps. Some are used as gantries for TV cameras to capture overhead shots at sporting events or for research purposes. Others operate simply as high-level advertising boards in the sky.

Takeoff and landing
When the Zeppelin takes off, its nose cone is detached from the mast truck. It lands by being manoeuvred into position alongside the mast and a cable is then attached to the nose. The cable is tightened and the Zeppelin is locked in place. A ground crew of just three people is required.

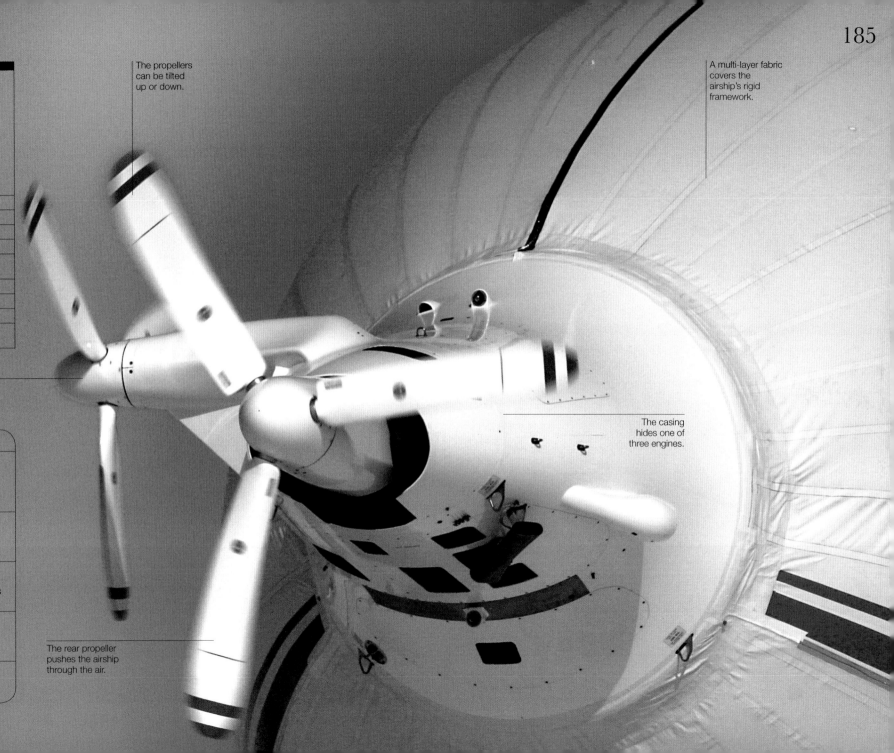

ZEPPELIN NT

Built in Friedrichshafen, Germany, the Zeppelin NT is used for various commercial missions and also operates tourist flights over Lake Constance. The cabin comfortably seats 12 passengers and includes a food galley and toilet facilities.

Specifications

Length: 75 m (246 ft)	
Width: 19.5 m (64 ft)	
Height: 17.4 m (57 ft)	
Balloon capacity: 8,225 cu m (290,474 cu ft) of nonflammable helium	
Passengers: 12	
Range: 900 km (559 miles)	
Top speed: 125 kph (78 mph)	
Maximum time in air without having to descend: 24 hours	

Airship trivia

■ The world's biggest airships were the *Hindenburg* and *Graf Zeppelin II*. Built in the 1930s, they measured 245 m (804 ft) in length and could travel at speeds up to 135 kph (84 mph).

■ Luxury airships from the 1920s included grand lounges, dining rooms, kitchens, passenger cabins, crew quarters, and observation decks.

■ A US company plans to build an airship similar in size to the airships of the 1930s, which will be able to carry 250 passengers nonstop for 9,660 km (6,000 miles).

■ High-altitude airships are being developed for use as telecommunication centres in the outer-atmosphere where bad weather cannot affect the signals.

■ Other designs for future airships include one for transporting cargo and another to fight forest fires.

The propellers can be tilted up or down.

A multi-layer fabric covers the airship's rigid framework.

The side propeller steers the airship on its chosen course.

The casing hides one of three engines.

The rear propeller pushes the airship through the air.

Free fall

Skydivers leap from planes and hurtle towards the ground at speeds of 200 kph (124 mph) or more. This is called free fall, where nothing slows their descent until they pull the rip cord and their parachutes open. Some skydivers perform set moves in a form of aerial gymnastics, while others use a skyboard to surf through the air with no force acting on the body except gravity. Bungee jumping is another activity that appeals to free-fall addicts, while hang-gliding offers a longer-lasting experience in the air.

Leap of faith
Once the plane door opens, the skydivers jump out one by one. First-timers usually dive from around 914 m (3,000 ft), which gives three seconds of free fall. The more adventurous dive from 3,350 m (10,990 ft) and enjoy 45 seconds of free fall. Experienced divers jump from even higher altitudes.

Air waves
With feet strapped to a skyboard, a skysurfer surfs, slides, spins, and twists in free fall. The display lasts about a minute, before the parachute is deployed. It is recorded on film by the surfer's co-jumper, who is known as the cameraflyer.

Piled high

For some skydivers, the acrobatics do not begin until their parachutes have been deployed. Parachute formation skydivers wear specially constructed parachutes that can be joined together in the air to form stacks or other shapes.

Precision landing

Parachute landing is a skill that involves aiming for a spot and reaching it with the body in the right position. There is a competitive skydiving category called "accuracy landing", where the skydiver tries to land on a 3-cm (1.25-in) target.

Elastic leap

With just an elastic harness attached to the torso or leg, bungee jumpers leap from cliffs, bridges, and buildings. Regulars master a variety of jump styles. A water touchdown involves dipping into water at the bottom.

Flying formations

Nicknamed "belly flying", formation skydiving is when teams of skydivers link up in the air and perform aerobatic displays. Competitive formation flying is done in teams of 4, 8, or 16. Recreational skydivers often jump in much larger groups, just for fun!

Hanging around

A glider is an unpowered aircraft. The hang-glider pilot hangs in a harness from the wing and uses a metal bar to control the glider and make the best use of air currents. Some pilots launch themselves off cliffs, while others are towed into the air by small, engine-powered planes.

Largest formation: 400 people (Thailand, 2006)   **Most people on a bungee rope:** 31 (Germany, 2000)   **Highest bungee jump from a building:** 180.1 m (590 ft 10 in) (New Zealand, 1998)

Huge helicopter
The world's biggest helicopter
is the Russian Mil Mi-26.
It is used by the air force to
transport troops and heavy
equipment. Also used by the
United Nations, the Mi-26 is
able to carry 63 passengers
or 20 tonnes of cargo.

Rotor power

Microlight
The smallest form of rotor-
powered flight is the microlight,
or ultralight. It consists of a
basic frame containing one or
two seats, with an engine behind
it and rotor blades above it.
Most microlights fly at speeds
less than 100 kph (62 mph).

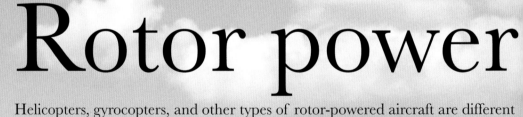

Helicopters, gyrocopters, and other types of rotor-powered aircraft are different
from fixed-wing planes because they can hover, take off vertically, and fly
backwards. It makes them more manoeuvrable than fixed-wing aircraft and
means they can land in far more difficult terrain. This is why helicopters are
the ideal form of transportation for military air forces and for humanitarian
missions, such as reaching remote areas affected by natural disasters.

Rotor facts

■ In 1480, Italian artist and inventor Leonardo da Vinci sketched an idea for a craft that would spin as it moved through the air. His "helical air screw" was one of the first-ever drawings of a helicopter.

■ Ukranian Igor Sikorsky developed what would be the first fully operational rotary-bladed helicopter in 1939. He later founded a successful helicopter manufacturing company that carried his name.

■ As well as being the world's largest helicopter, the Mil Mi-26 was also the first helicopter to use eight rotor blades.

■ Unlike a fixed-wing aircraft pilot, a helicopter pilot needs to use both arms and legs at the same time to fly the craft.

■ Tandem rotor helicopters, such as the US Chinook, have two main sets of rotor blades and no tail rotor.

■ Helicopters are used by a variety of professions, including the police, air ambulance services, and farmers.

■ There are more than 15,000 civilian helicopters in operation around the world.

Fast flier

Known as a slowed-rotor compound aircraft, the prototype CarterCopter uses a rotor to takeoff vertically like a helicopter, and a wing so it can fly at speeds of up to 805 kph (500 mph). However, it is not able to hover.

Clockwise chopper

One of the world's biggest helicopter makers, Eurocopter produces a range that includes the EC120. The rotor blades on Eurocopter craft turn clockwise, which is the opposite to all US-made craft, though the effect is exactly the same.

Cockpit controls

A helicopter pilot needs to control three things at the same time. The first is the collective control stick, which lifts or lowers the craft. The second is the cyclic control stick, which moves the helicopter forwards, backwards, and sideways. The third is the foot pedals, which control the angle of the tail rotor.

Rotor safety

Eurocopter developed the enclosed tail rotor, which features on all of its helicopters. Also known as a "fenestron", it is considered to be safer than traditional exposed rotor designs and is also more fuel-efficient.

1 The nose is one of a number of sections assembled in the "low hangar" area of the main building. Inner frame sections are put together and outer body panels are then fixed on to them. These sections are joined together to make the shell of the cockpit and nose.

5

Plane production

Building a luxury personal jet such as the Gulfstream G550 is a high-tech process. At the company's plant in Savannah, USA, the different elements of the plane, such as the fuselage, nose, and wings, are assembled separately before being joined together. It is a super-efficient assembly line – as soon as one section is finished, it moves along to the next team until, just 18 weeks later, the complete aircraft is ready to be tested and fitted out.

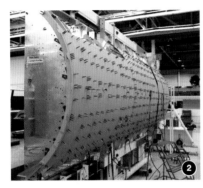

2 The fuselage is made up of three sections – forward, centre, and aft. These start off as flat panels and a machine bends them into a curved shape. They are then secured tightly, ready to be worked on.

3 After internal ribs have been added, three upper parts of the forward fuselage section are joined together. At the same time, other teams construct the centre and aft sections, nose, and tail.

4 The three fuselage sections are moved to the "high hangar" area of the building. Here, they are all joined to form one fuselage. The completed nose section is also added at this stage.

5 The wing sections arrive at the plant by rail and are joined together in the largest part of the main building. They are then fitted to the fuselage. The finished tail section is also attached to the aircraft.

6 The engines are delivered to Gulfstream in kit form. They are suspended in the air and then assembled. Once checked, the completed engine units are fitted to the fuselage.

7 The aircraft is moved to a test hangar. This is where everything apart from the engines and the auxilliary power unit is checked, including the plane's complex electronic systems.

8 After testing the engines, the aircraft is flown and receives its certificate of airworthiness. Finally, it is moved to the "completion centre" where it is painted and fitted out before being delivered to the buyer.

Angled fin blocks heat from the engine exhaust to prevent radar detection.

Clipped delta (triangular) wing is made of strong, lightweight titanium.

Each of the two weapons bays houses three missiles or a bomb.

The radar system is housed in Raptor's nose.

The inlet spike can be moved inwards to allow more air into the engine, which prevents damage from the shockwave produced when the plane breaks the speed of sound.

Engines generate more thrust than any other fighter aircraft.

Leading edge of horizontal stabilizer is at the same angle as front of wing.

War birds

Military aircraft are the most advanced flying machines in the world. Apart from spacecraft and rockets, they can travel faster and higher than anything else in the sky. Some incorporate "stealth" technology, which uses specialist construction materials and electronics to enable the aircraft to go undetected by other planes in the sky and radar on the ground. Pilots of jet fighters, bombers, and reconnaissance planes need to react quickly to cope with flying at up to three times the speed of sound. They are assisted by sophisticated computer displays that identify and track potential threats, and provide navigation information.

F-22A RAPTOR

The world's newest and most sophisticated supersonic fighter is the American F-22A Raptor. It combines stealth technology with exceptional thrust to create an aircraft that can fly virtually undetected at almost twice the speed of sound. The Raptor's powerful engines allow it to fly in "supercruise" mode. This means it does not need to waste fuel by using an afterburner to provide additional thrust.

Specifications	
Length	18.9 m (62 ft)
Wingspan	13.6 m (44 ft 6 in)
Wing area	78 sq m (840 sq ft)
Engine thrust	31,760 kg (70,000 lb)
Range	3,220 km (2,000 miles)
Top speed	2,413.5 kph+ (1,500 mph+)
Maximum altitude	15,235 m+ (50,000 ft+)

SR-71 BLACKBIRD

The Lockheed SR-71 Blackbird was one of the earliest aircraft to be designed to avoid radar detection. It first flew in 1964 and was so fast that if pilots detected a surface-to-air missile, they would simply accelerate to evade it. The Blackbird was the world's fastest operational aircraft until it was retired in 1998. It still holds the New York to London flight time record of 1 hour 55 minutes.

Specifications	
Length	32.74 m (107 ft 5 in)
Wingspan	16.94 m (55 ft 7 in)
Wing area	170 sq m (1,830 sq ft)
Engine thrust	29,480 kg (65,000 lb)
Range	5,926 km (3,680 miles)
Top speed	3,528.5 kph (2,193 mph)
Maximum altitude	25,910 m (85,000 ft)

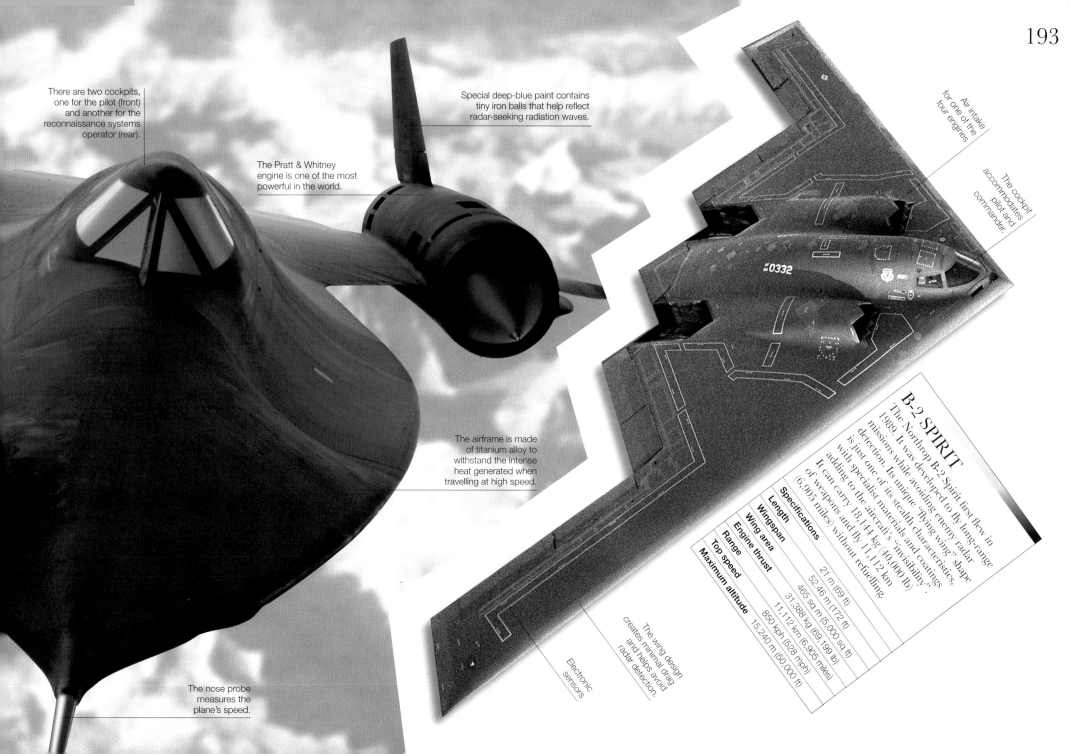

There are two cockpits, one for the pilot (front) and another for the reconnaissance systems operator (rear).

Special deep-blue paint contains tiny iron balls that help reflect radar-seeking radiation waves.

The Pratt & Whitney engine is one of the most powerful in the world.

Air intake for one of the four engines

The cockpit accommodates pilot and commander.

The airframe is made of titanium alloy to withstand the intense heat generated when travelling at high speed.

The wing design creates minimal drag and helps avoid radar detection.

Electronic sensors

The nose probe measures the plane's speed.

B-2 SPIRIT

The Northrop B-2 Spirit first flew in 1989. It was developed to fly long-range missions while avoiding enemy radar detection. Its unique "flying wing" shape is just one of its stealth characteristics, adding to the aircraft's "invisibility", with specialist materials and coatings.

It can carry 18,144 kg (40,000 lb) of weapons and fly 11,112 km (6,905 miles) without refuelling.

Specifications	
Length	21 m (69 ft)
Wingspan	52.46 m (172 ft)
Wing area	465 sq m (5,000 sq ft)
Engine thrust	31,388 kg (69,199 lb)
Range	11,112 km (6,905 miles)
Top speed	850 kph (528 mph)
Maximum altitude	15,240 m (50,000 ft)

At the controls

The flight deck of a modern airliner contains an array of visual displays, levers, and switches. The cockpit of this Airbus A330 also incorporates innovative side control-sticks that enable the pilot to bank, climb, or descend the plane. Pilots receive regular training to ensure that they fully understand the function of every lever and button.

Cockpit facts

■ Navigating a modern airliner involves using radio waves to plot route markers, although an increasing number of planes use GPS (Global Positioning System) to guide them.

■ In a traditional cockpit, there is one control column for the pilot and another for the co-pilot, so either can fly the plane.

■ Some airlines allow passengers to visit an aircraft's cockpit before or after – but never during – a flight.

■ Although an autopilot system can be used to fly a plane and land it, takeoffs are always carried out manually.

■ The pilot operates a mini steering wheel to direct the aircraft's nose wheel when it is taxiing on the ground.

■ Some planes can fly for up to three hours on one engine if the second one fails.

(1) The **Primary Flight Display** shows vital information such as air speed, banking, and barometric pressure.

(2) The **Navigation Display** shows the aircraft's position and course, which is plotted by an internal computer.

(3) Switches on the **Flight Control Unit** engage and disengage the autopilot, and also control speed.

(4) Engine data processed by a centralized monitor shows up on the **Primary Engine Display**.

(5) Additional engine information, including fuel use, is presented on the **Secondary Engine Display**.

(6) The **Multipurpose Control and Display Unit (MCDU)** displays the flight management system.

(7) The **Switching Panel** checks that the aircraft is configured correctly for takeoff.

(8) The **Thrust Control System** sets the engines to reverse idle, forward idle, climb, thrust, or take-off power.

(9) Controls for radio communications and frequency selection are on the **Radio Management Panel**.

(10) The **Audio Controls** contain radio- and public-announcement transmission panels and switches.

(11) Switches in the **Lighting Controls** operate the lighting systems in the aircraft's passenger cabin.

(12) The **Flap Lever** commands the positions of the flaps and wing slats during takeoff and landing.

Computerized controls

The A330 uses the same fly-by-wire computer technology first pioneered by Airbus on its A320 in 1988. This allows a pilot to input flight data into a central processing unit, which then controls the operation of the aircraft so that, essentially, the plane is able to fly by itself. It results in a safer form of flying because the onboard computers cannot exceed the predetermined limits set by the pilot.

13 The **Trim Selector** sets the rudder's neutral position and indicates the direction and extent of rudder trim.

14 Air brakes or wing spoilers to slow the aircraft for landing are operated by the **Speed Brake Lever**.

15 Fly-by-wire systems are controlled by the **Side Stick**, and are activated by pressing the red button.

16 For steering on the ground, the aircraft's nose wheel is turned by the **Nose Wheel Steering Tiller**.

17 The **Rudder Pedal** is a foot control used to turn the rudder and swing the tail to the left or right.

18 Situated between rudder pedals, the **Foot Rest** is used by the pilot while the plane is in autopilot mode.

19 The **Overhead Control Panel** houses emergency and oxygen systems, and a voice recorder.

20 A working **Tray Table** slides out from underneath the instrument panel over the pilot's lap.

21 Traditional "needle-and-dial" **Analogue Instruments** are used if the computer displays fail.

22 The **Captain's Seat** is always the left seat on a flight deck, and it slides back on tracks for access.

23 The **First Officer's Seat** is always the right seat on a flight deck, with duplicate controls and instruments.

24 If either of the two primary MCDUs fail, the **Back-up Multipurpose Control and Display Unit** is used.

Sky life

Each year, millions of people travel on passenger jets such as this Boeing 747. Soaring above the clouds at speeds of 912 kph (567 mph), the largest versions of these aircraft can carry more than 500 passengers and crew.

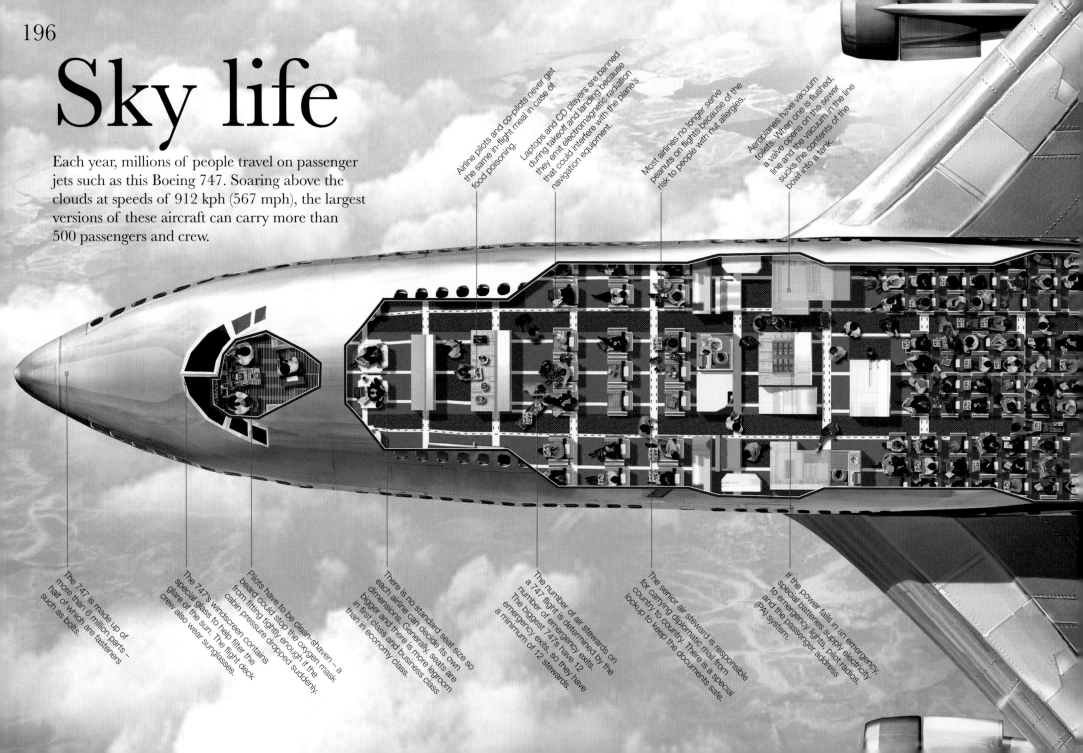

Airline pilots and co-pilots never get the same in-flight meal in case of food poisoning.

Laptops and CD players are banned during takeoff and landing because they emit electromagnetic radiation that could interfere with the plane's navigation equipment.

Most airlines no longer serve peanuts on flights because of the risk to people with nut allergies.

Aeroplanes have vacuum toilets. When one is flushed, a valve opens on the sewer line and the vacuum in the line sucks the contents of the bowl into a tank.

The 747 is made up of more than 6 million parts – half of which are fasteners such as bolts.

The 747's windscreen contains special glass to help filter the glare of the sun. The flight deck crew also wear sunglasses.

Pilots have to be clean-shaven – a beard could stop the oxygen mask from fitting tightly enough if the cabin pressure dropped suddenly.

There is no standard seat size so each airline can decide its own dimensions. Generally, seats are bigger and there is more legroom in first class and business class than in economy class.

The number of air stewards on a 747 flight is determined by the number of emergency exits. The biggest 747s have 12 emergency exits, so they have a minimum of 12 stewards.

The senior air steward is responsible for carrying diplomatic mail from country to country. There is a special lockup to keep the documents safe.

If the power fails in an emergency, special batteries supply electricity to emergency lights, pilot radios, and the passenger address (PA) system.

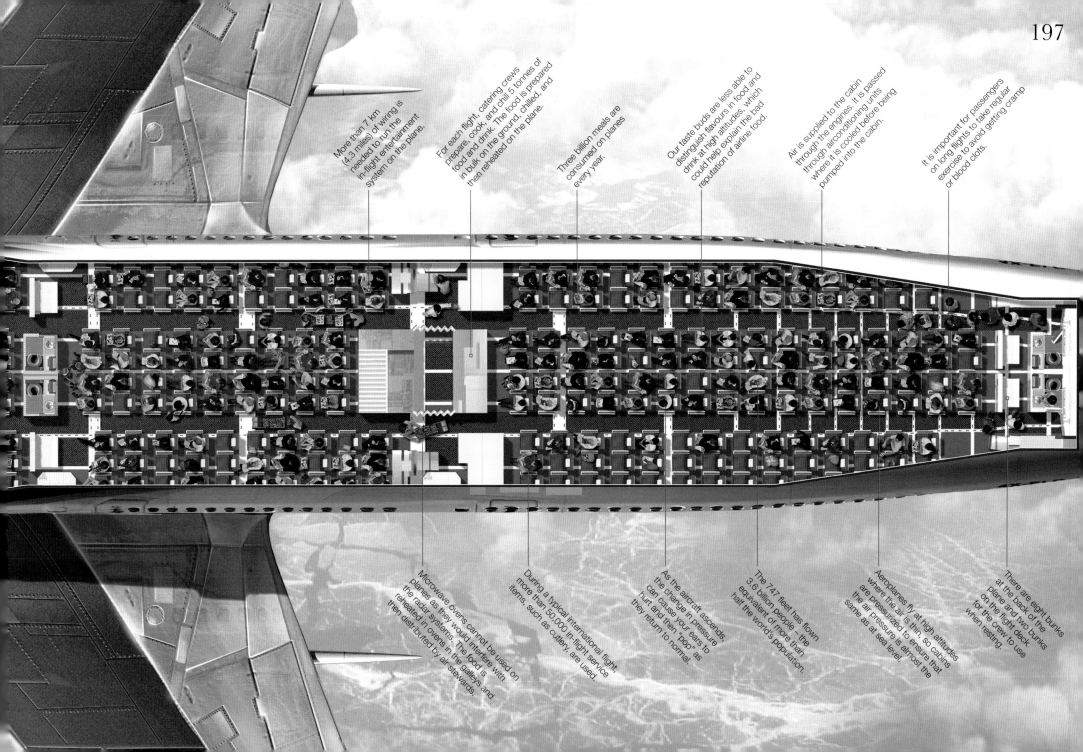

More than 7 km (4.3 miles) of wiring is needed to run the in-flight entertainment system on the plane.

For each flight, catering crews prepare, cook, and chill 5 tonnes of food and drink. The food is prepared in bulk on the ground, chilled, and then reheated on the plane.

Three billion meals are consumed on planes every year.

Our taste buds are less able to distinguish flavours in food and drink at high altitudes, which could help explain the bad reputation of airline food.

Air is supplied to the cabin through the engines. It is passed where it is cooled before being pumped into the cabin.

It is important for passengers on long flights to take regular exercise to avoid getting cramp or blood clots.

Microwave ovens cannot be used on planes as they would interfere with the radar systems. The food is reheated in ovens in the galleys and then distributed by air stewards.

During a typical international flight more than 50,000 in-flight service items, such as cutlery, are used.

As the aircraft ascends, the change in pressure can cause your ears to hurt and then "pop" as they return to normal.

The 747 fleet has flown 3.6 billion people – the equivalent of more than half the world's population.

Aeroplanes fly at high altitudes where the air is thin, so cabins are pressurized to ensure that the air pressure is almost the same as at sea level.

There are eight bunks at the back of the plane and two bunks on the flight deck for the crew to use when resting.

Giant in the sky

The Airbus A380 is the largest passenger airliner in the world, capable of carrying more than 850 people. The parts that make up the aircraft are produced at locations all over the globe. They are then transported by land, sea, and air to the main A380 plant at Toulouse in France. Here, the giant double-decker aircraft is assembled and tested before being flown to Hamburg, Germany, to be fitted out and painted in the airlines' brand colours.

By sea

A specially built ship transports sections of the plane's fuselage from Hamburg, Germany, to Mostyn in Wales, where the A380's wings are collected. The ship then travels to St Nazaire in France. Here, more fuselage sections are loaded on before the ship sails to its final destination near Bordeaux, France.

By air

Vertical tailplane sections for the A380 are manufactured in Stade, Germany. From there, the 14.1-m- (46.3-ft-) tall tails are loaded onto an Airbus Beluga transporter aircraft and flown to Toulouse, France.

By road

After the ship has docked near Bordeaux, the fuselage, wings, and tailplane parts are loaded onto barges. These travel down to Langon, France, where the A380 parts are unloaded and placed on specially adapted trailers for the road journey to Toulouse. To minimize disruption, the lorries travel only at night.

First in line

In May 2004, the first A380 came off the final assembly line in Toulouse. It was then moved to another hangar where it began its testing programme. This process took two years and included testing the aircraft in extreme weather conditions.

NETHERLANDS
BELGIUM
SWEDEN
FINLAND
RUSSIA
UK
POLAND
GERMANY
CZECH REPUBLIC
AUSTRIA
SWITZERLAND
FRANCE
ITALY
TURKEY
SPAIN
MOROCCO

USA
CANADA

KEY

△ A380 suppliers
■ Airbus manufacturing sites

Worldwide operation

As well as the 16 main Airbus manufacturing sites in Europe, there are many other suppliers across the world. In addition to those shown above, suppliers are also located in Australia, Japan, Malaysia, and South Korea.

Final destination

The A380's final assembly plant in Toulouse was built especially for the new aircraft. The building is 500 m (1,640 ft) long, 250 m (820 ft) wide, and 46 m (151 ft) high. As well as the main assembly building there is also a separate ground testing hangar.

Inflight testing

The A380 made its maiden flight in April 2005 and received safety certificates from both European and US air authorities in March 2006. Even after this, the A380 still had to undergo 2,500 hours of inflight safety testing. Five aircraft were used for this purpose, with two of them specifically testing things such as aerodynamics, vibration, and the effects of low-speed flying.

Top terminals

Many factors have influenced the growth of air travel, including advances in aviation technology, the expansion of international trade, and the increased affordability of flying. It is now possible to fly to virtually anywhere in the world in under 24 hours. Much of the world's population lives in the northern hemisphere, so most major passenger routes operate in this region.

Air has also become an important method of transporting freight around the world, especially low-weight goods of high value. Many of the main cargo airports are located on principal international trade routes, such as between Asia and the USA.

This map illustrates the top ten busiest passenger and cargo airports in 2005, as well as the largest passenger airports in Africa, Australasia, and Latin America. The takeoff and landings figures include both passenger and cargo flights for each airport.

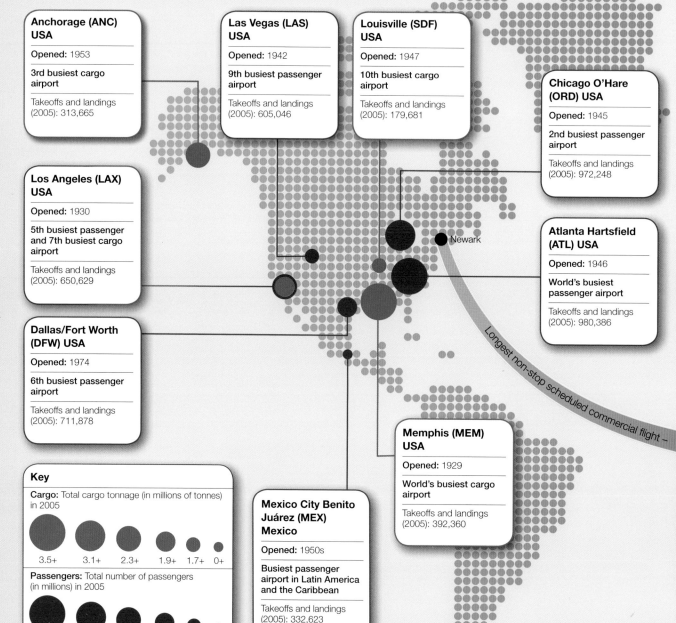

Anchorage (ANC) USA
Opened: 1953
3rd busiest cargo airport
Takeoffs and landings (2005): 313,665

Las Vegas (LAS) USA
Opened: 1942
9th busiest passenger airport
Takeoffs and landings (2005): 605,046

Louisville (SDF) USA
Opened: 1947
10th busiest cargo airport
Takeoffs and landings (2005): 179,681

Chicago O'Hare (ORD) USA
Opened: 1945
2nd busiest passenger airport
Takeoffs and landings (2005): 972,248

Los Angeles (LAX) USA
Opened: 1930
5th busiest passenger and 7th busiest cargo airport
Takeoffs and landings (2005): 650,629

Atlanta Hartsfield (ATL) USA
Opened: 1946
World's busiest passenger airport
Takeoffs and landings (2005): 980,386

Dallas/Fort Worth (DFW) USA
Opened: 1974
6th busiest passenger airport
Takeoffs and landings (2005): 711,878

Newark

Longest non-stop scheduled commercial flight –

Memphis (MEM) USA
Opened: 1929
World's busiest cargo airport
Takeoffs and landings (2005): 392,360

Mexico City Benito Juárez (MEX) Mexico
Opened: 1950s
Busiest passenger airport in Latin America and the Caribbean
Takeoffs and landings (2005): 332,623

Key

Cargo: Total cargo tonnage (in millions of tonnes) in 2005
3.5+   3.1+   2.3+   1.9+   1.7+   0+

Passengers: Total number of passengers (in millions) in 2005
80+   70+   60+   50+   40+   0+

London Heathrow (LHR) England

Opened: 1946

3rd busiest passenger airport

Takeoffs and landings (2005): 477,888

Amsterdam Schiphol (AMS) Netherlands

Opened: 1920

10th busiest passenger airport

Takeoffs and landings (2005): 420,633

Frankfurt Main (FRA) Germany

Opened: 1936

6th busiest cargo and 8th busiest passenger airport

Takeoffs and landings (2005): 490,147

Seoul (ICN) South Korea

Opened: 2001

5th busiest cargo airport

Takeoffs and landings (2005): 163,575

Tokyo Narita (NRT) Japan

Opened: 1978

4th busiest cargo airport

Takeoffs and landings (2005): 189,498

Airport codes

There are two types of codes used to identify airports around the world. The first is based on a system set up by the International Air Transport Association (IATA) and is made up of three letters. These codes are used for airline timetables and to identify the origin and destination of passengers' baggage. The second type is a four-lettered International Civil Aviation Organization (ICAO) code. This variety is more comprehensive and includes not only an abbreviation for the airport, but also indicates the region where it is located. The ICAO code is used by air traffic controllers and increasingly by airlines.

Tokyo Haneda (HND) Japan

Opened: 1931

4th busiest passenger airport

Takeoffs and landings (2005): 295,745

Paris Charles de Gaulle (CDG) France

Opened: 1974

7th busiest passenger airport

Takeoffs and landings (2005): 522,619

Shanghai (PVG) China

Opened: 1999

8th busiest cargo airport

Takeoffs and landings (2005): 205,045

Singapore (SIN) Singapore

Opened: 1981

9th busiest cargo airport

Takeoffs and landings (2005): 208,280

Newark to **Singapore** (18–20 hours)

Johannesburg (JIA) South Africa

Opened: 1952

Busiest passenger airport in Africa

Takeoffs and landings (2005): 197,335

Hong Kong (HKG) China

Opened: 1998

2nd busiest cargo airport

Takeoffs and landings (2005): 273,407

Sydney Kingsford Smith (SYD) Australia

Opened: 1920

Busiest passenger airport in Australasia

Takeoffs and landings (2005): 286,827

Air travel

■ About three-quarters of all air traffic operates within and between three regions: Asia, Europe, and North America

■ The world's busiest air route is across the North Atlantic.

■ Flying is more affordable than it ever has been. Developments in technology mean that, in real terms, average air fares are cheaper now than they were in the 1970s.

■ Poland, China, and the Czech Republic are among the countries predicted to experience major growth in international passenger traffic up to 2009.

■ In the same period, China (along with Asia-Pacific countries such as Thailand and Malaysia) is predicted to have the biggest expansion in international freight traffic.

■ Memphis is the world's busiest cargo airport because it is the home of FedEx. UPS has its international headquarters at Louisville, the 10th busiest air cargo hub.

■ The world's biggest airport in terms of area is Riyadh in Saudia Arabia – it covers approximately 225 sq km (87 sq miles).

The passengers

Kansai International is a busy airport – more than 16 million passengers used it in 2005. It means there is a constant flow of people in the terminal, from those waiting to board flights to others who have just disembarked their aircraft.

Koji
Koji travelled an hour from Kagoshima to take pictures of aircraft. "The Kansai terminal is beautiful."

Hiromi
Hiromi is having a massage while waiting for a flight. "The first time I came to Kansai I thought the architecture was wonderful."

Setsuko
Setsuko is going on holiday with her husband Asani. "We travelled to the airport by train and are catching a plane to Okinawa."

Shirakashi family
"This is our first visit to Kansai International Airport. We came to show our two children the planes taking off and landing."

Gilbert
Gilbert is an engineer from Australia returning after a business trip. "Kansai is very modern and clean."

At the airport
The first floor of Kansai's airport terminal is for international arrivals. Domestic flights are on the second floor, shops and restaurants are found on the third floor, and international departures check in on the fourth floor.

Terminal trivia

■ Around 45,000 passengers pass through the airport each day.
■ At 1.7 km (1.06 miles) long, the airport terminal is the largest in the world.
■ The roof is covered with 82,000 steel panels.

■ The arched roof is specially designed to channel fresh air from one side of the terminal to the other.
■ Supporting columns under the terminal can be adjusted if there is any land movement.

■ A bridge connects the airport to the mainland to provide road and rail connections. Travellers can also arrive by high-speed ferry.
■ Passengers are transported through the airport by people-conveyers and lifts.

■ At the top of the airport terminal is the Aeroplaza, a complex containing shops and the island's only hotel.
■ A second runway is planned to enter service in 2007.

Lying 5 km (3.1 miles) off the coast of Honshu, Japan, is an artificial island. It was constructed to provide an offshore location for Kansai International Airport. The airport's distance from residential areas means it can operate around the clock. Every day thousands of passengers pass through the long, wing-shaped terminal building.

Kansai International Airport
Osaka

Durable building
The terminal building is constructed to withstand earthquakes and typhoon winds.

The workers

From porters to check-in staff, security men to cleaners, the airport employs an army of different workers to ensure that travellers' needs are met. Many jobs operate around the clock, ensuring the smooth running of the airport 24/7.

Eiji and Yukitaka

Pilot Eiji and his co-pilot Yukitaka work for All Nippon Airways. "We both like to fly Boeing 747s."

Shiori

Air stewardess Shiori works for All Nippon Airways and flies all over Japan. "My favourite route is to Ishigaki Island in the south."

Junzo

Junzo works in the Legend of Concorde restaurant. "The most popular meal is a replica of the food served on board the aircraft."

Kazuko

As one of the airport cleaners, Kazuko works in a team of 30 people. "I enjoy meeting all the foreign people here."

Teruko

Teruko has worked as a radar operator at Kansai for eight years. "The view of the airport in the ocean is something special."

Keizo

Trolley operator Keizo started working at the airport soon after it opened in 1995. "This is a very friendly place to work."

Susumu

Maintenance worker Susumu carries out preflight and arrival checks on aircraft during the day. "On the night shift, I do periodic maintenance and general repairs on the aircraft."

People power

■ It took 10,000 labourers three years to construct the artificial island upon which the airport is located. The 30-m (98-ft) layer of foundations required rock and earth to be excavated from three mountains.

■ Hundreds of staff are needed to work in the airport's 35 restaurants. Most of them serve Japanese food such as sushi and noodles. In addition, there are 26 coffee shops and bars, and 110 shops.

■ International flights from Kansai go to 72 cities in 29 different countries.
■ Kansai also has connections to 14 domestic cities, including Tokyo Haneda, Sapporo, and Kagoshima.

■ Its location means that Kansai is the only airport in Japan allowed to operate at night.
■ For visitors wanting to know more about Kansai's history and construction, official guides offer tours of the airport.

Plane spotting

From small, single-seater light aircraft to super-airliners that can carry more than 850 people, the skies are filled with many types of civilian planes. Airports are the best place to spot them, especially the more popular commercial airliners, but most planes flying overhead can be identifed by their wing profile, engine position, and tail shape.

AIRBUS A380-800

The world's largest civilian airliner has two decks and a wing that weighs in at 750 tonnes. Some versions of the A380 are able to carry up to 853 passengers.

Specifications

Length	73 m (239 ft 6 in)
Wingspan	79.8 m (261 ft 9 in)
Cruising speed	955 kph (593 mph)
Passengers	Up to 853

BOEING 747-400

The most successful wide-body jet in history, the 747 is continually being upgraded. The 747-400 has raised wing tips for improved aerodynamics, as well as a new flight deck.

Specifications

Length	70.6 m (231 ft 7 in)
Wingspan	64.4 m (211 ft 4 in)
Cruising speed	912 kph (567 mph)
Passengers	Up to 524

AIRBUS A340-600

The longest commercial airliner in the world, the A340-600 is used on long-haul routes. As well as transporting passengers, it has a large cargo-carrying capacity.

Specifications

Length	75.30 m (247 ft)
Wingspan	63.45 m (208 ft 2 in)
Cruising speed	923 kph (573 mph)
Passengers	Up to 419

ILYUSHIN IL-96M

The Il-96 first flew in the early 1990s and is one of Russia's most advanced airliners. The M is longer than earlier types and can travel nonstop for 10,400 km (6,462 miles).

Specifications

Length	64.7 m (212 ft 3 in)
Wingspan	60.11 m (197 ft 3 in)
Cruising speed	830 kph (516 mph)
Passengers	Up to 375

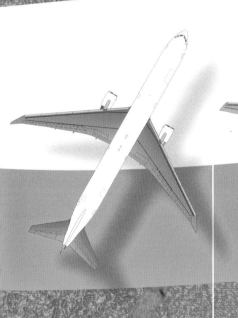

BOEING 767-400

The 767 is often used for crossing the Atlantic Ocean. It has flown this route more times than all other aircraft types combined. The 400 has the longest fuselage in the 767 range.

Specifications	
Length	61.4 m (201 ft 5 in)
Wingspan	51.9 m (170 ft 3 in)
Cruising speed	851 kph (529 mph)
Passengers	Up to 375

BOEING 737-700

Making its first flight in 1968, the Boeing 737 is in the record books as the most highly produced jet airliner ever. When the range was revamped in 1993, the 737-700 was introduced.

Specifications	
Length	33.6 m (110 ft 3 in)
Wingspan	34.3 m (112 ft 6 in)
Cruising speed	851 kph (529 mph)
Passengers	Up to 149

AIRBUS A320-200

The first passenger airliner to use computer technology to fly a plane, the A320 set new standards when it was unveiled in 1988. It remains a popular short-range aircraft.

Specifications	
Length	37.57 m (123 ft 3 in)
Wingspan	34.09 m (111 ft 9 in)
Cruising speed	870 kph (541 mph)
Passengers	Up to 164

GULFSTREAM G400

The G400 is a high-specification business jet that can carry eight passengers in ultimate luxury. It is able to travel as fast as many commercial airliners.

Specifications	
Length	26.9 m (88 ft 3 in)
Wingspan	23.7 m (77 ft 9 in)
Cruising speed	850 kph (528 mph)
Passengers	Up to 8

CESSNA CARAVAN

One of the world's most successful light aircraft, the Caravan can be used for a variety of purposes including passenger transportation and carrying cargo.

Specifications	
Length	11.5 m (37 ft 7 in)
Wingspan	15.9 m (52 ft 2 in)
Top speed	341 kph (212 mph)
Passengers	Up to 14

Air identity

From the early days of commercial passenger flight, airlines realized how important it was to have a strong corporate identity. In a competitive market, it made their brand stand out and could attract potential customers. The most visible

place to display a design is across the tailplane, which can be seen from the ground when an aircraft is up in the air. Other methods of promoting airline identity include colourful advertising posters and designer uniforms for the crew.

Tailplanes

Whether simply displaying the name or livery of an airline or illustrating a more elaborate motif such as the British Airways example above, tailplanes are the most important and prominent identity space on an aircraft.

SAS tail (1970s)

United Airlines tail (1930s)

Air France tail (1950s)

United Airlines advertising (1930s)

FASTEST · SHORTEST · FAIR TO FAIR

Lufthansa advertising (1960s)

Promotional material

Airlines use advertisements to attract customers. Images of exotic destinations, details of on-board services, and information about special offers are used to target potential passengers.

Air France advertising (1950s)

The MacMichaels fly to Italy on the world's largest airline

He's William MacMichael of Sherman, Texas, a production manager of a factory equipment. She's Betty Jane. And the boy is Tommy, their twelve old son. Why did they choose Air France to Italy? Too many reasons to list here. But to name a direct jets to Paris from Houston (Air France also has jet flights from New York, Chicago, Los Ang and other cities). Ideal connections in Italy. (Air France serves more cities in Europe with jets than any other airline.) Fabulous food. (It's French!) Incomparable service. (It's French!) jet fares. (Note lower on any other airline.) Now what's your reason for flying Air France this y

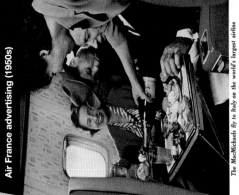

AIR FRANCE

Air France uniform (2005)

In-flight fashion

Airlines dress their crew in smart clothes, with flight attendants wearing uniforms in the colour of the airline. Some airlines will provide forms of local dress for their crew — female Air India crew, for example, wear saris on flights. Others commission famous designers to create their uniforms. In 2005, Air France asked the world-renowned designer Christian Lacroix to come up with the airline's new uniforms.

LUFTHANSA

Deutsche Lufthansa advertising (1930s)

DEUTSCHE LUFT HANSA

D-1310

British Airways advertising (2000s)

BRITISH AIRWAYS HOLIDAYS

British Overseas Airways Corporation (BOAC) uniform (1950s)

B.O.A.C

United Airlines uniform (1960s)

Pie in the sky

Physical changes to the human body when flying in a plane mean that a lot of thought has to go into creating airline meals. During a flight, air pressure affects the taste buds in your mouth so that your sense of taste diminishes.

In addition, flying at altitude dehydrates the body, so only low levels of salt, which itself dehydrates, can be used. Food is prepared on the ground and then transferred to the aircraft before being reheated in the galleys and served up.

Preparing the food
Every day, hundreds of thousands of meals are prepared for air travellers around the world. Methods to ensure that the food tastes good in the air include slow-simmering, which retains more nutrients than if cooked at normal speed, and pressure-cooking, where meals are cooked, vacuum-packed, and then placed into ice-cold water to retain their freshness. Techniques such as deep-frying are avoided because they do not reheat well.

Loading up

The kitchens are usually located near to airports so that the food does not need to travel far to the aircraft. Most in-flight food companies also incorporate refrigeration facilities where meals can be kept fresh before being loaded onto the aircraft. Once in the plane, the food is moved into storage containers situated in the galley. The airline crew will then reheat the food before serving it up to the passengers.

Dining in style

As well as comfortable seats with plenty of leg room, first- and business-class passengers receive top-quality food served on china plates. Even though the preparation techniques are the same as for economy-class food, final presentation touches are often added by the stewards. Passengers can select what they want to eat from a comprehensive menu, which can include duck, veal, or lobster, washed down with complimentary fine wines.

Standard fare

Airlines provide different menus depending on what class ticket a passenger has bought. On long-haul flights, some airlines will offer a choice of two main meals, and there is often a salad and bread roll included as well. A vegetarian option or other specialist meal can be ordered, but the airline needs to be informed at least 24 hours before the flight. The packaging, plates, and cutlery in economy class are usually made of plastic.

Ralph the Robot

Design for Chunks

In 2001, a design company invited a number of designers to decorate sick bags with their own individual artwork. It was such a success that it turned into an annual event. In 2004, the 20 best sick bags from the fourth Design for Chunks competition were featured on Virgin Atlantic's flights for six months.

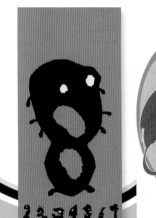

pukewpet

Sick bags

Air-sickness bags used to be functional objects found inside aircraft seat pockets, but they have now developed into a specialist art form. Some have even become collectors' items, with rare bags fetching hundreds of pounds in on-line auctions.

ZOOK!

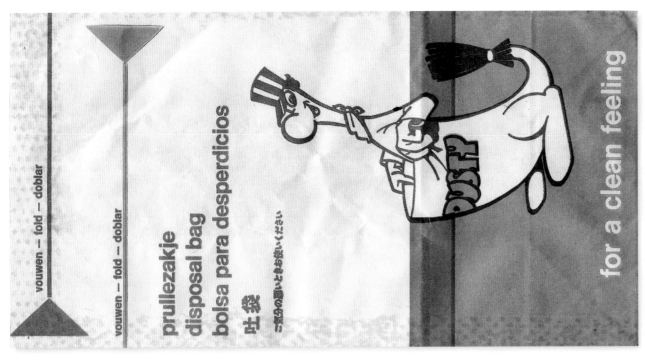

vouwen — fold — doblar

vouwen — fold — doblar

prullezakje
disposal bag
bolsa para desperdicios
吐袋

for a clean feeling

Cabin collectables
For collectors, sick bags like this "Dusty the Kangaroo" example made by KLM in 1983 are highly prized. Even more valuable are bags dating from before 1970 and those produced by airlines that are no longer in business, such as Pan Am, Trans World Airlines (TWA), and Sabena.

The science of air sickness

■ Air sickness is a type of motion sickness. It is caused when, during irregular movement, the brain gets confused by mixed signals from sensors (especially in the inner ear and eyes) that indicate the position of the body. It is most likely to occur while an aircraft is going through turbulence.

■ Symptoms of air sickness include nausea, vomiting, sweating, headaches, and a loss of colour in the cheeks.

■ Only certain people are susceptible to air sickness, but it is not known why they are more prone than others.

■ Ways of avoiding air sickness before getting on an aircraft include carrying out specific exercises and wearing a wrist band that acts on a pressure point. For those who suffer badly, medication can be prescribed to calm the inner ear and prevent imbalance.

■ Tips for helping prevent air sickness while on a plane include choosing a seat over the wing – the most stable part of the aircraft in flight – and focusing on distant objects rather than close ones. It is better to look out of the window than to read a book or watch a film.

Lined for strength
Most sick bags come in a standard rectangular shape and are made of paper with a thin plastic or wax interior lining. Swissair produces a bag that can also be used as an envelope to send camera films off to be developed.

AIR CHINA   AEROFLOT   SWISSAIR   AIR INDIA   CATHAY PACIFIC   KOREAN AIR   KLM

CARGO

Air transport is much quicker than sending goods by sea. Some cargo planes are owned by airlines specializing in freight, while others are part of bigger, passenger-carrying fleets. These planes have transformed people's lives. Thanks to them, nothing is more than 24 hours away. Day and night, planes travel the skies with holds full of urgent mail or perishable goods such as fruit, vegetables, and exotic flowers.

Air freight facts

■ FedEx is the world's biggest transport company. Its cargo airline, FedEx Express, is based in Memphis, Tennessee, USA.

■ In 2003, the FedEx "Panda Express" transported two giant pandas from Beijing, China, to Memphis Zoo, USA.

■ The American firm United Parcel Service (UPS) delivers more than 15 million packages around the world each day.

■ British Airways' Perishable Handling Centre (PHC) deals with more than 80,000 tonnes of fresh produce every year.

■ Perishables make up 11 per cent of all air freight in terms of weight.

■ About 70 per cent of all the perishables that enter the USA arrive at Miami airport.

■ NASA's Super Guppy can carry a maximum load of 24,700 kg (54,454 lb).

Loading up
No other aircraft has a fuselage as high as the Airbus Beluga's and none can match its cargo capacity. The plane's "forehead" lifts up to reveal a 1,400-cu m (49,440-cu ft) cargo bay that can carry large aircraft parts and International Space Station components.

Airbus Beluga
Named after the Beluga whale on account of its size and shape, this aircraft was built specifically to transport components for Airbus airliners to assembly plants across Europe. Airbus is jointly owned by French, British, German, and Spanish aerospace companies.

Nonstop operation
Besides fruit, vegetables, and flowers, other time-sensitive cargoes include seafood and pharmaceuticals. They are transported in temperature-controlled containers. Planes also carry mail (private, business, and diplomatic), pets, and even human organs for use in transplants. Rail and road connections at airports ensure that products reach their destinations as quickly as possible.

Customs and paperwork
Only packages that are being transported by a national postal service carry stamps. Private freight companies directly charge or bill the sender instead. All packages must carry the correct documentation, which is checked by customs officials at airports. Most companies give packages a barcode label, too, so that its location can be tracked at any time.

264 9479 431

Cargo carrier
Founded in 1971, the FedEx Corporation now flies parcels to more than 220 countries and territories around the world. Its fleet of around 700 aircraft is backed up by 43,000 vans, cars, and motorcycles. The company can transport packages between major cities in a matter of hours. Between 2008 and 2011, FedEx will take delivery of ten Airbus A380 freighters, the world's largest cargo planes.

Super Guppy
The US space agency, NASA, uses an aircraft called the Super Guppy to move International Space Station components and other outsize cargo items. Based on a military Boeing aircraft, the Super Guppy has a hinged nose that opens for easy loading and a 7.6-m- (25-ft-) wide fuselage. The aircraft also has rails and rollers in its cargo bay that can be used to secure and move pallets.

DHL WPX
website http://www.dhl.com

AO OAA LAMBETH, UNITED KINGD

C

Shipment No.
Sender's reference : 2649479431
CHRIS STOWERS

MAY 2005

ORIG

SORT.

LON

AIRWAYBILL:
26494794

Light aircraft

The Zodiac XL is a kit plane. It can be built with totally separate components or by using a quick-build kit where some sections are preassembled. Because many parts have already been cut and riveted, only basic tools are needed to put the plane together – on average, it takes less than 500 hours to build. And you can then take to the air to enjoy your handiwork!

Plane in a box

Apart from the engine and instrument dials, all the Zodiac XL's parts are shipped in a wooden crate. To help buyers build the plane, a manual CD is included, containing instructions, photos, graphs, and technical drawings.

Customizing the plane

Buyers can choose a number of different options, including a range of engines from 100 to 125 horsepower, two- or three-bladed propellers, and a choice of vinyl or leather seats.

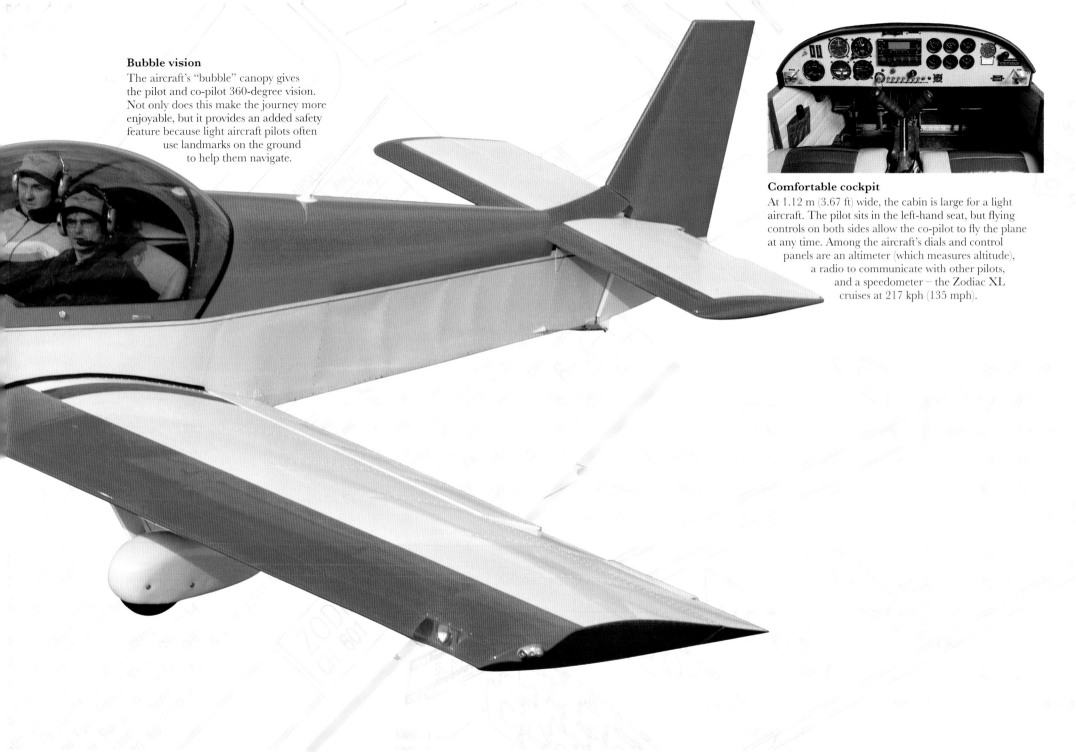

Bubble vision
The aircraft's "bubble" canopy gives the pilot and co-pilot 360-degree vision. Not only does this make the journey more enjoyable, but it provides an added safety feature because light aircraft pilots often use landmarks on the ground to help them navigate.

Comfortable cockpit
At 1.12 m (3.67 ft) wide, the cabin is large for a light aircraft. The pilot sits in the left-hand seat, but flying controls on both sides allow the co-pilot to fly the plane at any time. Among the aircraft's dials and control panels are an altimeter (which measures altitude), a radio to communicate with other pilots, and a speedometer – the Zodiac XL cruises at 217 kph (135 mph).

Managing the skies

In the USA alone, about 75,000 aircraft take off from airports every day, with many thousands more passing through the country's air space. This is why the work of air traffic controllers is vital to keep planes from colliding in midair. Some controllers work in towers at airports to coordinate aircraft taking off and landing, while others are based in regional centres where they monitor aircraft en route to their destinations.

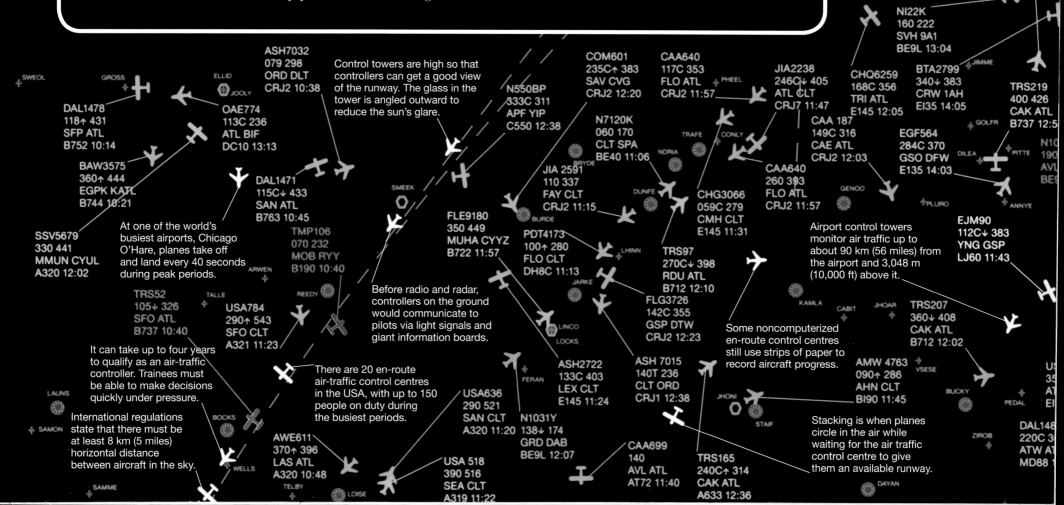

It takes between one and four minutes for an aircraft to land and leave a runway, allowing about 30 landings an hour.

Radar technology was first invented in 1922, but it was not until the 1950s that it had developed enough for use in air-traffic control.

Control towers are high so that controllers can get a good view of the runway. The glass in the tower is angled outward to reduce the sun's glare.

At one of the world's busiest airports, Chicago O'Hare, planes take off and land every 40 seconds during peak periods.

Before radio and radar, controllers on the ground would communicate to pilots via light signals and giant information boards.

It can take up to four years to qualify as an air-traffic controller. Trainees must be able to make decisions quickly under pressure.

International regulations state that there must be at least 8 km (5 miles) horizontal distance between aircraft in the sky.

There are 20 en-route air-traffic control centres in the USA, with up to 150 people on duty during the busiest periods.

Airport control towers monitor air traffic up to about 90 km (56 miles) from the airport and 3,048 m (10,000 ft) above it.

Some noncomputerized en-route control centres still use strips of paper to record aircraft progress.

Stacking is when planes circle in the air while waiting for the air traffic control centre to give them an available runway.

AAL1225 300 397 RDU DFW MD82 14:25

DAL656 330↓ 478 ATL EWR MD88 13:36

NI22K 160 222 SVH 9A1 BE9L 13:04

BTA2799 340↓ 383 CRW 1AH EI35 14:05

TRS219 400 426 CAK ATL B737 12:5

ASH7032 079 298 ORD DLT CRJ2 10:38

COM601 235C↑ 383 SAV CVG CRJ2 12:20

CAA640 117C 353 FLO ATL CRJ2 11:57

JIA2238 246C↓ 405 ATL CLT CRJ7 11:47

CHQ6259 168C 356 TRI ATL E145 12:05

DAL1478 118↑ 431 SFP ATL B752 10:14

OAE774 113C 236 ATL BIF DC10 13:13

N550BP 333C 311 APF YIP C550 12:38

N7120K 060 170 CLT SPA BE40 11:06

CAA 187 149C 316 CAE ATL CRJ2 12:03

EGF564 284C 370 GSO DFW E135 14:03

BAW3575 360↑ 444 EGPK KATL B744 10:21

DAL1471 115C↓ 433 SAN ATL B763 10:45

JIA 2591 110 337 FAY CLT CRJ2 11:15

CAA640 260 393 FLO ATL CRJ2 11:57

EJM90 112C↓ 383 YNG GSP LJ60 11:43

SSV5679 330 441 MMUN CYUL A320 12:02

FLE9180 350 449 MUHA CYYZ B722 11:57

PDT4173 100↑ 280 FLO CLT DH8C 11:13

CHG3066 059C 279 CMH CLT E145 11:31

TMP106 070 232 MOB RYY B190 10:40

TRS97 270C↓ 398 RDU ATL B712 12:10

TRS52 105↓ 326 SFO ATL B737 10:40

USA784 290↑ 543 SFO CLT A321 11:23

FLG3726 142C 355 GSP DTW CRJ2 12:23

TRS207 360↓ 408 CAK ATL B712 12:02

ASH2722 133C 403 LEX CLT E145 11:24

ASH 7015 140T 236 CLT ORD CRJ1 12:38

AMW 4763 090↑ 286 AHN CLT BI90 11:45

USA636 290 521 SAN CLT A320 11:20

N1031Y 138↓ 174 GRD DAB BE9L 12:07

AWE611 370↑ 396 LAS ATL A320 10:48

CAA699 140 AVL ATL AT72 11:40

TRS165 240C↑ 314 CAK ATL A633 12:36

USA 518 390 516 SEA CLT A319 11:22

DAL148 220C 3 ATW AT MD88 1

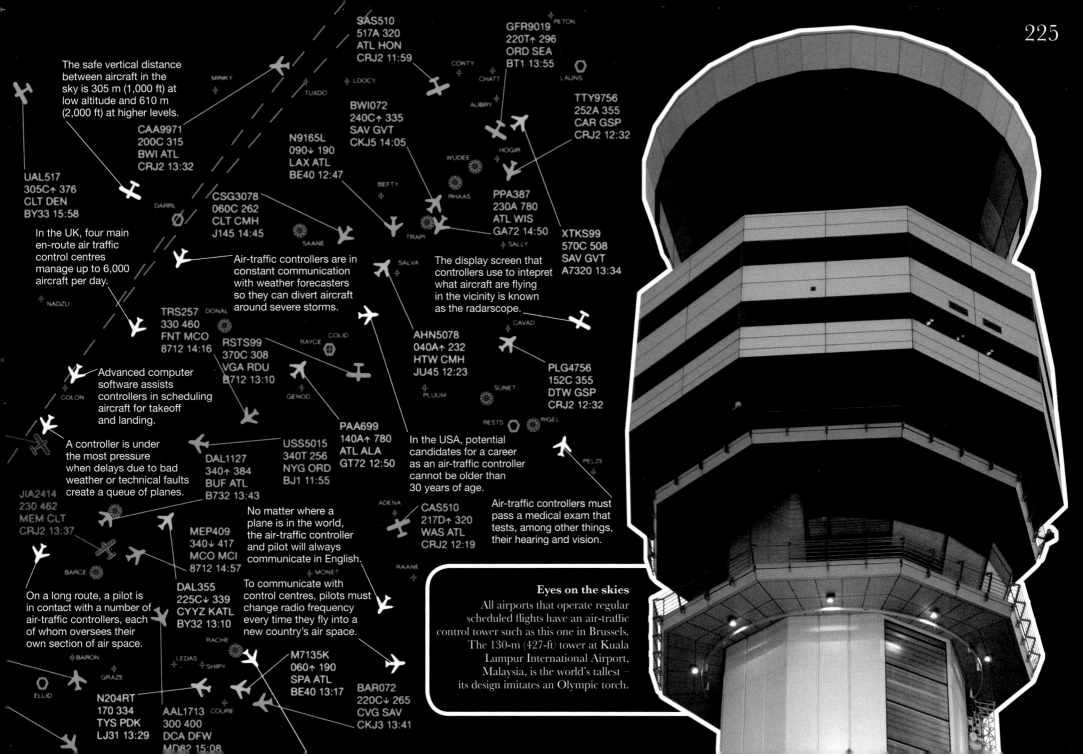

The safe vertical distance between aircraft in the sky is 305 m (1,000 ft) at low altitude and 610 m (2,000 ft) at higher levels.

In the UK, four main en-route air traffic control centres manage up to 6,000 aircraft per day.

Air-traffic controllers are in constant communication with weather forecasters so they can divert aircraft around severe storms.

The display screen that controllers use to interpret what aircraft are flying in the vicinity is known as the radarscope.

Advanced computer software assists controllers in scheduling aircraft for takeoff and landing.

A controller is under the most pressure when delays due to bad weather or technical faults create a queue of planes.

In the USA, potential candidates for a career as an air-traffic controller cannot be older than 30 years of age.

Air-traffic controllers must pass a medical exam that tests, among other things, their hearing and vision.

No matter where a plane is in the world, the air-traffic controller and pilot will always communicate in English.

On a long route, a pilot is in contact with a number of air-traffic controllers, each of whom oversees their own section of air space.

To communicate with control centres, pilots must change radio frequency every time they fly into a new country's air space.

Eyes on the skies

All airports that operate regular scheduled flights have an air-traffic control tower such as this one in Brussels. The 130-m (427-ft) tower at Kuala Lumpur International Airport, Malaysia, is the world's tallest – its design imitates an Olympic torch.

SAS510 517A 320 ATL HON CRJ2 11:59

GFR9019 220T↑ 296 ORD SEA BT1 13:55

TTY9756 252A 355 CAR GSP CRJ2 12:32

BWI072 240C↑ 335 SAV GVT CKJ5 14:05

N9165L 090↓ 190 LAX ATL BE40 12:47

CAA9971 200C 315 BWI ATL CRJ2 13:32

UAL517 305C↑ 376 CLT DEN BY33 15:58

CSG3078 060C 262 CLT CMH J145 14:45

PPA387 230A 780 ATL WIS GA72 14:50

XTKS99 570C 508 SAV GVT A7320 13:34

TRS257 330 460 FNT MCO 8712 14:16

RSTS99 370C 308 VGA RDU B712 13:10

AHN5078 040A↑ 232 HTW CMH JU45 12:23

PLG4756 152C 355 DTW GSP CRJ2 12:32

PAA699 140A↑ 780 ATL ALA GT72 12:50

USS5015 340T 256 NYG ORD BJ1 11:55

DAL1127 340↑ 384 BUF ATL B732 13:43

JIA2414 230 462 MEM CLT CRJ2 13:37

CAS510 217D↑ 320 WAS ATL CRJ2 12:19

MEP409 340↓ 417 MCO MCI 8712 14:57

DAL355 225C↓ 339 CYYZ KATL BY32 13:10

M7135K 060↑ 190 SPA ATL BE40 13:17

BAR072 220C↓ 265 CVG SAV CKJ3 13:41

N204RT 170 334 TYS PDK LJ31 13:29

AAL1713 300 400 DCA DFW MD82 15:08

Space tourism

In one giant leap for tourism, companies are producing commercial spacecraft to take people into space. Since space flights began in the 1960s, only about 500 astronauts have travelled beyond Earth's atmosphere. This figure is set to rocket as new types of craft take off and the cost of space travel drops. Budding astronauts won't need to undergo months of intensive training – several days of preflight simulation and medical screenings will be all it takes to reach the final frontier.

Prized possession

The Ansari X Prize was devised in 1996 to encourage low-cost commercial space travel. The US$10 million (£5.4 million) prize was for the first nongovernment organization to launch a reusable piloted craft into space twice in a fortnight. On 4 October 2004, the Tier One Project group won with *SpaceShipOne*.

Blast off!

Around the world, 26 teams took part in the Ansari X Prize competition. Starchaser Industries successfully launched the privately built rocket *Nova* in 2001. However, it was unmanned and reached a height of 1.68 km (1.04 miles), far short of the 100 km (62 miles) necessary to win the prize.

Launch of space tourism

US businessman Dennis Tito was the world's first space tourist. In April 2001, he paid US$20 million (£10.8 million) to board the *Soyuz TM-32* spacecraft. He spent 7 days, 22 hours, and 4 minutes in orbit, and docked at the International Space Station.

In the driving seat

The cockpit of *SpaceShipOne* is surrounded by a protective outer shell to ensure that any problems with the craft will not lead to loss of cabin pressure. The craft has strategically placed windows to give the pilot multiple views of the horizon. These windows have to be small to minimize the weight of the vehicle.

Spaced out

A number of companies provide astronaut training and one even offers zero-gravity flights on an adapted Ilyushin Il-76 aircraft. State-of-the-art technology produces realistic simulation so that passengers can experience weightlessness without actually travelling into space.

The Galactic's adjustable wings adopt a "shuttlecock" shape when re-entering Earth's atmosphere so that the craft drifts slowly and gently back down.

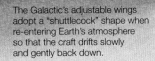

Inside the craft, passengers will be able to release their safety straps and float around the cabin to experience weightlessness.

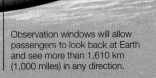

Observation windows will allow passengers to look back at Earth and see more than 1,610 km (1,000 miles) in any direction.

Checking into orbit

Although this hotel is only an artist's impression, holidays in space could become a reality. Space Island Project plans to connect empty space shuttle fuel tanks and create a space hotel.

Beyond the stars

Virgin Galactic, part of British entrepreneur Sir Richard Branson's Virgin Group, is planning space travel for the masses. By offering affordable flights to paying passengers, a trip to space could become as commonplace and hassle-free as boarding an aeroplane. The fleet of spacecraft are based on the Ansari X Prize-winning *SpaceShipOne* design.

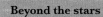

Air junk

From broken Boeings to battered B-52 bombers,
all aircraft eventually come to the end of their
useful lives. When planes are no longer able to fly,
they are transported to specialist "graveyard" sites
where they are broken up. In space, there is another type of junk as hundreds
of thousands of pieces that have fallen off rockets and satellites circle the
orbits of Earth and other planets. Although small, these bits of debris pose
a threat to active space missions and need to be constantly monitored.

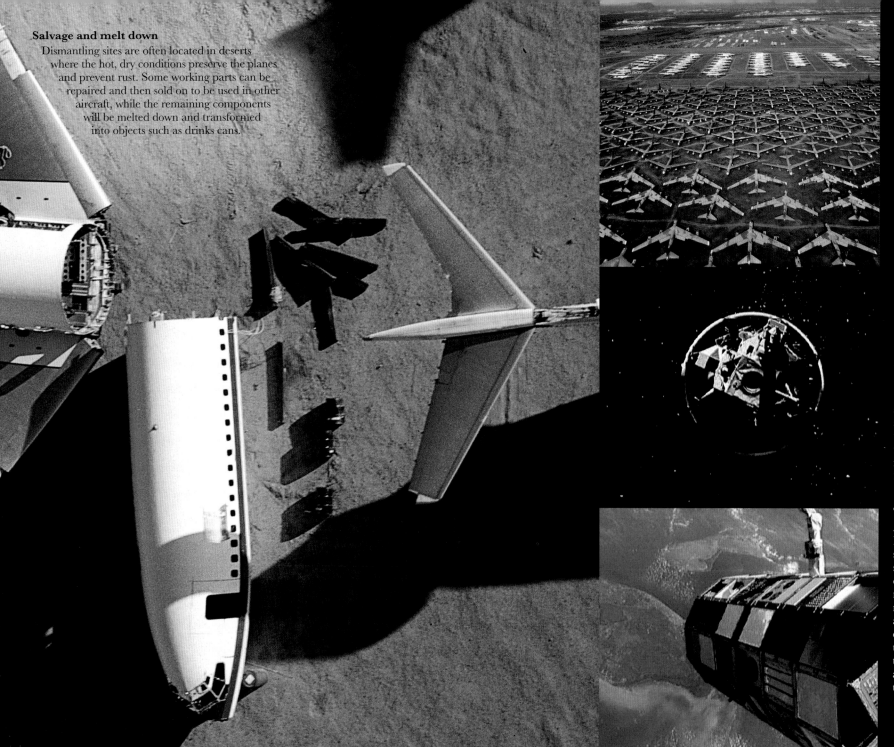

Salvage and melt down

Dismantling sites are often located in deserts where the hot, dry conditions preserve the planes and prevent rust. Some working parts can be repaired and then sold on to be used in other aircraft, while the remaining components will be melted down and transformed into objects such as drinks cans.

Military graveyard

More than 5,000 old fighters and bombers, mainly B-52s, are stored at the Davis Monthan Air Force base in Arizona, USA. Some are scrapped, others are kept for their spare parts, while a few are transformed into "drones". These small planes do not have pilots but are flown by remote control, and on-board cameras are used to take pictures of the ground.

Space junk

There are an estimated one million pieces of artificial debris floating out in space. Many, such as those surrounding this Lunar Module, are created by spacecraft after they separate from the rockets that take them out into space. Even though most space junk is no bigger than a pebble, it is a threat to spacecraft because it is travelling at about 28,000 kph (17,398 mph).

Testing for debris

A spacecraft called the Long Duration Exposure Facility spent almost six years in space carrying out a number of experiments. One measured the amount of meteorite particles and artificial debris in Earth's orbit. The mission concluded that about 40 per cent of the debris in low orbit was artificial, a much higher figure than had been expected.

Record highs

Most aircraft landings in 24 hours
In May 2001, American Thomas Bishop made 442 takeoffs and landings in his light aircraft at an airfield in Texas, USA, over a 24-hour period.

Fastest jet
In 1964, the two-seat high-speed US military jet called the Blackbird flew in excess of Mach 3.0 – three times the speed of sound.

Busiest passenger airport
The world's busiest airport is Atlanta Hartsfield, USA, which dealt with 85,905,000 passengers and had 980,386 takeoffs and landings in 2005.

Longest time spent in a hot-air balloon
In 1999, Englishman Brian Jones and Swiss Bertrand Piccard flew around the world, setting off from Switzerland and landing in Egypt 19 days, 21 hours, and 47 minutes later.

Oldest wing-walker
Born on 21 August 1912 in Zimbabwe, William Green did a wing-walk 88 years, 10 months, and one week later. This record-breaking wing-walk took place in South Africa on 14 July 2001.

Largest passenger aircraft
Launched in 2000 and set to enter service in 2007, the Airbus A380 is 73 m (239 ft 6 in) long and has a wingspan of 79.8 m (261 ft 9 in). It will be able to carry over 850 passengers.

Most aircraft taking off in one hour
On 10 September 2004, Dutchman Meine Brethouwer celebrated his wedding anniversary by arranging for 87 aircraft to take off in one hour from Holland's Lelystad Airport.

Most parachute descents
By the end of 2005, American Don Kellner had made more than 36,000 free fall skydives. His first parachute jump was 44 years earlier.

Highest hot-air balloon altitude
On 6 June 1988, Per Lindstrand flew his Colt 600 hot-air balloon up to a height of 19,811 m (64,997 ft) over Texas, USA.

From packed passenger planes to heavy helicopters, hot-air balloons to paper aeroplanes, wing-walkers to sky-divers, the record books are packed with high-flyers. And with more and more people taking to the skies, either looking for thrills or purely for travel purposes, some of these records may be broken, while others will be created.

Largest model aeroplane collection
From 1936 up until his death in 2003, American John Kalusa had constructed 5,829 wooden aeroplanes. The collection is housed at the Embry-Riddle Aeronautical University in Arizona, USA.

Most aircraft flown in as a passenger
In 1943, Englishman Edwin A Shackleton went on his first flight in a De Havilland DH 89. By July 2004, he had flown in 806 different types of aircraft, including airships, hot-air balloons, and microlights.

Fastest circumnavigation on scheduled flights
In January 1980, Englishman David J Springbett circumnavigated the globe in 44 hours and 6 minutes. His 37,124-km (23,068-mile) trip started and finished in Los Angeles and involved eight flights.

Longest paper aeroplane flight
American Ken Blackburn hand-launched his paper aeroplane at the Georgia Dome, Atlanta, in October 1998 – it stayed aloft for 27.6 seconds.

Fastest microlight flight around the world
Englishman Colin Bodill qualified as a microlight instructor in 1980. He became a recordbreaker in 2000 after flying around the world in 99 days.

Largest helicopter
The world's largest helicopter is the five-seat Russian Mil Mi-26. It is 40 m (131 ft) in length and has a maximum takeoff weight of 56,000 kg.

Fastest propeller-driven aircraft
The Soviet Tu-95/142 can travel at a top speed of 925 kph (575 mph). This incredible speed is achieved by four powerful turboprop propellers, each driving huge eight-blade propellers.

Largest airship
This record is shared by two airships (Graf Zeppelin II [LZ 129] and the German Hindenburg [LZ 130]) – both airships measured 245 m (803 ft 10 in) long.

Most scheduled flights in 24 hours
In 1990, Englishman Michael Bartlett made 42 scheduled flights with Heli Transport between Cannes, Nice, and Sophia Antipolis.

The wing-like fin is designed to help the skydiver glide along on air currents.

Future travel

Flight of fancy

In 2003, Austrian Felix Baumgartner took the sport of skydiving to a futuristic level. With a 1.8-m- (6-ft-) long carbon-fibre fin strapped to his back, he leapt from a plane and rode air currents for 35 km (22 miles), crossing the English Channel.

Driverless cabs

A pilot scheme of a driverless taxi system is underway in Cardiff, Wales. The computer-controlled ULTra pods collect passengers from pick-up points and then travel along elevated rail networks to a passenger's chosen destination.

The pod is designed to carry four passengers, with two seats at the front and rear.

Made of fibreglass, each cab's payload weighs 500 kg (1,103 lb).

The world of transport is constantly evolving, with new designs and prototypes pushing technological boundaries. Coping with congested urban areas, developing solutions to the problem of a depleting fuel supply, and finding ways to visit the previously unexplored parts of our planet are the driving forces behind much of the innovation. In the space of just a few years, a new idea can become a reality and the technology a commonplace feature of our everyday lives.

Annual number of air travel passengers: 2 billion

Largest planned cruise ship: Royal Caribbean are building 360-m (1,181-ft) cruise ship that can carry 5,400 passengers

Predicted number of cars in the world by 2035: More than 850 million

Ocean flyer

Powered by two propellers, the Deep Flight Aviator is a submersible that literally flies through ocean water. It can dive at speeds of around 100 m (328 ft) per minute, which is faster than any other submersible. Rudders at the back of the craft allow it to rotate sideways, so the pilot can explore the ocean depths.

Propellers drive the craft forwards at speeds up to 14.8 kph (9.2 mph).

The cabs travel along a purpose-built, 1.6-m- (5.3-ft-) wide elevated track.

The battery-powered ULTra cabs travel at an average speed of 39.6 kph (24.6 mph).

Fare paid by first space tourist: Dennis Tito paid US$20 million (£11,405,000) for his 2001 space flight

Passenger fare on Virgin Galactic's first suborbital flight in 2007: Each space tourist will pay US$200,000 (£114,000) for their space journey

Urban transporter

Designed to be used in pedestrian areas, the Segway HT is a two-wheeled transportation device. Electrically powered, the rider stands on a platform and controls the self-balancing Segway using the handles. A nifty device for getting around urban areas, it has been tested in the USA by police on patrol.

A flat tyre can cause the car to express sadness by glowing blue.

Mood car

Japanese company Toyota has developed a car that shows feelings. The driver's voice, pulse, and perspiration levels are monitored to gauge emotions and the front of the POD car lights up in different colours to indicate mood. If the car glows red for anger, soothing music is played to the driver.

234

On the GO!

It has been quite a journey making this book. In fact, the total distance the team travelled was 187,561 km (116,545 miles), which is almost five times the circumference of the Earth! We sent photographers to many different countries to take pictures of boats, car towers, airports, stunt riders, kit planes, and much more. We clocked up thousands more kilometres commuting to and from work every day. The book's journey continued after our work was finished. Packed into a container ship, it travelled from Hong Kong to reach bookshops and other outlets all over the world.

Tracks and tyres

We clocked up nearly 2,000 bus trips, more than 3,000 train journeys, 24 flights, 120 car rides, 60 motorbike rides, and 10 ferry trips – not to mention a considerable distance by foot.

 24 60 3000 2000 10 120 1

1 Mexico, Missouri, USA
After photographing every part of a Zodiac XL plane, the team got to fly in one.

2 Savannah, Georgia, USA
The ease with which these Gulfstream planes were put together was recorded.

3 New York City, USA
We spent three days at Grand Central Terminal talking to staff and commuters.

4 Dakar, Africa
As the Dakar Rally drivers raced across Africa, we followed their route.

5 Exeter, UK
Motorcross rider Jason Smyth dazzled us with spectacular stunts.

6 Southampton, UK
We watched a racing sailboat being assembled and photographed its parts.

7 London, UK
Staff and commuters on the London Underground network gave us their views.

181561 kilometres   116545 miles

8 Hannover, Germany
The incredible Car Towers
we visited are part of
a motoring theme park.

9 Dresden, Germany
We photographed the
assembly line at Volkswagen's
Gläserne Manufacktur.

10 Bologna, Italy
Ducati let us reduce one of
their racing motorbikes into
its component parts.

11 Delhi, India
Travelling on buses all over
Delhi gave us a unique view
of the city.

12 Sydney, Australia
For the photoshoot on the
Sydney ferries, having good
sea legs was an advantage.

13 Osaka, Japan
The sleek architecture is
why we chose a feature on
Osaka Airport.

14 Hong Kong, China
The printed books were
packed into containers and
shipped from Hong Kong.

Index

Index

Acknowledgements

DK would like to thank:
Idris Ahmed, Andy Crawford, Jim Green, Barry Hayden, Dave King, David Mager, Kenny McLeish, and Chris Stowers for photography; Darren Robert Awauh and Mark Longworth for illustrations.

Niki Foreman, Hoa Luc, and Kate Scarborough for editorial assistance; Joe Conneally and Jim Green for design assistance; Indexing Specialists (UK) Ltd, Hove, for the index.

Mark Ledington from the Morgan Motor Company; Bartosz Piechota and Craig Outhwaite from Evans Cycles, Waterloo Road, London; Ludovica Benedetti, Massimo Davoli, and Livio Lodi at Ducati, Bologna; Sebastien Heintz, Roger Dubbert, Hick Heintz, and all the staff at Zenith Aircraft Company; Alex Southon, Rob Britton, Jim Hood, and RS Racing for the use of an RS700. For further details on the RS range visit www.rssailing.com; Jason Smyth, motocross stuntman. See www.adrenaline.tour.com; Nichola Batten at the Volkswagen Autostadt, Wolfsburg; Alexander Skibbe at the Gläserne Manufaktur, Dresden; GoinGreen for use of Reva G-Wiz. For more information see www.goingreen.co.uk; Daniel M Brucker at Grand Central Terminal; Valerie Buckingham and Taiyaba Khatoon for help organizing the Delhi photoshoot; Laura Wallace and the Emergency Response Unit team at Vauxhall, London; Belinda Luton and Ann Laker from the London Underground Press Office and Shirley Cody from the Film Liaison Office; Daisuke Komine from Kansai International Airport Co., Ltd; Tomoko Matusi from All Nippon Airways Co., Ltd; Kenji Makino from Kansai International Airport Office, Osaka Regional Civil Aviation Bureau, Ministry Of Land, Infrastructure, and Transport; Keiko Yokoh, Nicolas Dhuez, and Yumiko Tahata for help with the Kansai Airport photoshoot; Carol Wiley for interviewing passengers and staff of Sydney Ferries; the team at Sydney Ferries; Robert Baugniet, Julie McCoy, and all the staff at Gulfstream; Steve McMahon from Aerosite.net; Mark Jackson from Slam City Skates, London; Selina Da Silva from the 100 Marathon Club; Maria Aurura Hinayon from Airports Council International; Marcus Hutchinson from America's Cup; Debbi Gibbs and Steve Bailey from Gibbs Aquada; Michael Gallagher at Cunard for *QM2* queries.

The publisher would like to thank the following for their kind permission to reproduce their photographs:
(Key: a-above; b-below/bottom; c-centre; l-left; r-right; t-top)

1 SuperStock: age fotostock/Javier Larrea. 3 SuperStock: age fotostock/Brian Bielmann. 4 SuperStock: age fotostock/Liane Cary. 6-7 SuperStock: age fotostock/G.V.P. 8-9 Bluegreen Pictures. 10 The Art Archive: Dagli Orti (1/b). Bridgeman Art Library: Royal Thames Yacht Club, London, UK (5/b). © The Trustees of the British Museum: Chas Howson (2/b); Ivor Kerslake (2/t). DK Images: Judith Miller/Sloans & Kenyon (4/b); courtesy of the National Maritime Museum, London/James Stevenson & Tina Chambers (3/t) (3/b). Exeter Maritime Museum, the National Maritime Museum London: (1/t). © National Maritime Museum, London: James Stevenson (5/t). 10-11 Corbis: Rick Doyle (background). 11 Corbis: Bettmann (2/t) (3/b); MacDuff Everton (5/t); Reuters/Henny Ray Abrams (5/b). 12 Alamy Images: Sami Sarkis (tr). Corbis: Peter Guttman (br). Eye Ubiquitous: Marcus Wilson-Smith (l). World Pictures: (c). 12-13 Alamy Images: Blackout Concepts/Mark Owen (background). 13 Camera Press: Gamma/Bertrand Rieger (bl). Corbis: Sygma/Christophe Delattre (br). Panos Pictures: Mark Henley (tr). SuperStock: age fotostock/Doug Scott (tr). Courtesy of US Navy: JO1 Joseph Krypel (c). 14 Alamy Images: Andy Hallam (tc). Getty Images: The Image Bank/Sakis Papadopoulos (b). Courtesy of US Navy: PH2 (AW) Jonathan R. Kulp (tr). 14-15 Kos Picture Source: Kris. 15 Bluegreen Pictures: Christian Février (b). 16-17 courtesy Hapag-Lloyd. 18 Alamy Images: Roger Bamber. 19 Alamy Images: Jiri Rezac (br). Getty Images: National Geographic/Randy Olson (t); Taxi (tc). Hyundai Heavy Industries: (bl). Reuters: Lee Jae-Won (tr). Courtesy of US Navy: (bc). 20 Alamy Images: G.P. Bowater (l); nagelstock.com (r). Getty Images: Yngve Rakke (cb). Fred Olsen Production AS: (ca). 20-21 Corbis: Gary Braasch (background). 21 Alamy Images: Kos Picture Source (tl). Corbis: Denis Balibouse (tr). Getty Images: Stone/David Frazier (c). SuperStock: Jon Warden (bl). 22 The Art Archive: Culver Pictures (bl). Camera Press: Gamma/Gilles Mermet. Corbis: Dave G. Houser (br). Getty Images: Hulton Archive (bc/right). Reuters: Eliana Aponte (bc/left). 23 Corbis: (br). Reuters: (bc). SuperStock: Hubertus Kanus (c). 24 Getty Images: The Image Bank/Richard A. Brooks (l). Still Pictures: Ron Giling (r). 25 Alamy Images: LeighSmith Images (c). DK Images: Gerald Lopez (r).

Still Pictures: Ron Giling (l). 27 Corbis: Dennis Degnan. 32-33 Bluegreen Pictures: Rick Tomlinson. 33 Harvie Allison, www.harvpix.com: (b). Rex Features: Verity Reily Collins (c). courtesy, U.S. Coastguard: PA2 Andy Devilbiss (c). 34 Alamy Images: Dan Burton (tr); Buzz Pictures (b); Stephen Frink Collection (2). Corbis: Eye Ubiquitous/David Cumming (1); Karen Kasmauski (3). Crescent Hydropolis Resorts PLC: (4). Photolibrary: Mark Webster (5). 34-35 Oceanwide Images. 35 Corbis: Bettmann (10); Yogi, Inc (8). FLPA: Minden Pictures/Norbert Wu (tc). NOAA: (9). Photolibrary: Gerard Soury (cb). Science Photo Library: Alexis Rosenfeld (7). 36-37 Reuters. 37 Empics Ltd: AP/Bob Child (tr) (br). Courtesy of US Navy: Chief Photographer's Mate John E. Gay (cr). 38 Courtesy of US Navy: PH1 Brien Aho (l). USS George Washington and the U.S. Navy/ Gary Ombler: (r/all). 39 USS George Washington and the U.S. Navy/ Gary Ombler. 41 SuperStock: Jorge Alvarez (l). 48 Reuters: Paul Pelissier. 49 Corbis: Sygma/Guillaume Plisson (b); Onne van der Wal (t). 50-51 Kos Picture Source: ACM/SEA&SEE/Carlo Borlenghi. 51 Empics Ltd: DPA (br). 52 Guido Grugnola: (tr). Gilles Martin-Raget: (bl). 52-53 Gilles Martin-Raget. 53 Guido Grugnola: (b). Gilles Martin-Raget: (tc) (tr). courtesy, 118 WallyPower: (cr) (br). 54 Corbis: David Lees (bl). Mary Evans Picture Library: (tr) (cr) (br). courtesy, NYK Cruises: (b). 54-55 Mary Evans Picture Library: (background). 55 The Advertising Archives: (cla) (clb). The Art Archive: Chris Deakes/Private Collection (cl). Empics Ltd: DPA (cr); Fiona Hanson (t). Getty Images: The Image Bank/Larry Gatz (crb). P&O Cruises: (r) (l/centre) (b). Photolibrary: foodpix (cra). 56-57 Corbis: zefa/Pete Leonard (background). courtesy, Cunard Line. 58-59 All photos courtesy of Gibbs Technologies. 60 Corbis: Rick Doyle. 61 Action Plus: Tom Hauck (cl); Philippe Millereau (bl). Alamy Images: Jon Arnold Images/James Montgomery (cb). Corbis: Steve Wilkings (tl). Getty Images: The Image Bank/Ryan McVay (tr); Stone/Brian Bailey (b). 62 Alamy Images: Travelshots.com (l). Imagestate: Hoa-Qui/Jeremy Horner (r). 63 Alamy Images: Carole Hewer (b). SuperStock: age fotostock/Javier Larrea (t). World Pictures: (tr). Aspasia Coumiotis: (l). 64-65 Alamy Images: David Kilpatrick. 65 Camera Press: Gamma/Raphael Gaillarde (t). DK Images: Rough Guides/Victor Borg (r). Photos: Klaus Frahm; Design:von Gerkan, Marg und Partner, Architects: (c). Graeme Peacock, www.graeme-peacock.com: (bl) (bc). 66-67 Alamy Images: David Robertson. 68-69 SuperStock: age fotostock/Angelo Cavalli. 70 Corbis: Alex Steedman (3/t). DK Images: Courtesy of the Motorcycle Heritage Museum, Westerville, Ohio (4/b); Courtesy of the National Motor Museum, Beaulieu (5/b); Courtesy of The Science Museum, London (1/t); Courtesy of The Science Museum, London/Clive Streeter (1/b); Courtesy of The Science Museum, London/ Mike Dunning (2/t). Science & Society Picture Library: (5/t). 70-71 Corbis: ChromoSohm Inc./Joseph Sohm (background). 71 Action Plus: Richard Francis (4/t). Alamy Images: Motoring Picture Library (5/t). Corbis: Paul Almasy (3/b); Reuters/John Hillery (5/b). DK Images: (c) Imperial War Museum, London/Andy Crawford (1/b); Courtesy of the National Motor Museum, Beaulieu (2/t); Courtesy of Slam City Skates (3/t). Robert Harding Picture Library: Nigel Francis (4/b). Science & Society Picture Library: (1/t). 73 Empics Ltd: PA/Niall Carson (tr). 80-81 Masterfile: Peter Griffith. 86 Alamy Images: Motoring Picture Library (r). Corbis: (cr). Getty Images: Hulton Archive/David Savill (c). TopFoto.co.uk: HIP (l). 86-87 Rex Features: Charles M. Ommanney (b). 87 Reuters: (t). 88 DK Images: National Motor Museum (ca/Mercedes 300SL). 96 courtesy of Reva Electric Car Company Pvt Ltd, www.goingreen.co.uk. 97 Corbis: Reuters/John Hillery (r). Getty Images: AFP/Kazuhiro Nogi (c); courtesy of Reva Electric Car Company Pvt Ltd, www.goingreen.co.uk: (tl) (bl) (c). 98 Alamy Images: PCL (br). Volkswagen: (bl) (bc. 99 Courtesy of Autostadt GmbH, Wolfsburg, Germany: (bl). Roger Gorringe: (bc/right). The Kobal Collection: Walt Disney Pictures/Richard Cartwright (bc/left). Volkswagen: (br). 100 Art Directors & TRIP: Warren Jacobs (l). 101 Alamy Images: David Wall (c). Camera Press: Gamma/Gilles Bassignac (r). Getty Images: National Geographic/Raymond K. Gehman (tl); Panoramic Images (cla); Stone/Robert Van Der Hilst (bl). Panos Pictures: Dermot Tatlow (clb). 102 Alamy Images: Gari Wyn Williams (l). Corbis: Benjamin Rondel (l). Getty Images: Taxi/Michael Hart (bc). 103 Alamy Images: Anthony Brown (r); Iain Masterton (r); Photo Japan (r); Gari Wyn Williams (clb) (br). Art Directors & TRIP: Keith Cardwell (tc). Corbis: Murat Taner (bl). Getty Images: The Image Bank/Grant Faint (cl). 104 Alamy Images: Pat Behnke (bl). Getty Images: Stone/Will & Deni McIntyre (tl). Paul Vlaar, paul@neep. net: (r). 105 Action Plus: Andy Day (l). Alamy Images: George Blonsky (tr).

Getty Images: The Image Bank/John William Banagan (br). 112 Alamy Images: Chris P. Batson (tl); David Gordon (b/Glasgow); Megapress (b/Mexico City); Natalie Pecht (b/Buenos Aires); Robert Harding Picture Library Ltd/Sylvain Grandadam (b/Berlin). Camera Press: Scanpix/Tone Georgsen (b/Oslo). Masterfile: Steve Craft (b/Toronto). Rex Features: Andrew Drysdale (b/Budapest); Sipa Press (r). 113 Alamy Images: Iain Masterton (tl); Robert Harding Picture Library Ltd/Sylvain Grandadam (b/St Petersburg); Neil Setchfield (b/Singapore); TNT Magazine (tc); Visual & Written SL/Kike Calvo (b/Hong Kong); Colin Walton (b/Melbourne). Corbis: Reuters/Lee Jae-Won (b/Pyongyang); David Sailors (b/Cairo). Panos Pictures: Paul Smith (b/Kolkata). Rex Features: JD/Keystone USA (tr). 114 Alamy Images: AW Photography (t/Hong Kong); Pat Behnke (c/Brussels); Robert Fried (b/Madrid); Cris Haigh (c/Bangkok); Nic Hamilton (t/Prague); Jon Hicks (t/Singapore); Iain Masterton (t/Moscow) (b/Osaka); Beren Patterson (b/Buenos Aires); Marco Regalia (c/Lisbon); Neil Setchfield (c/Tokyo); Jack Sullivan (c/Vienna); Peter Titmuss (t/Rotterdam). Camera Press: Scanpix/Jens Noergaard Larsen (t/Copenhagen); TSPL/Robert Perry (c/Rome). Corbis: B.S.P.I. (b/Stockholm); David Sailors (b/Los Angeles). Masterfile: Bryan Reinhart (b/Salzburg). 115 Alamy Images: StockAbcd (br). Art Directors & TRIP: (t). Camera Press: Gamma/S009 (r/Pyongyang); Gamma/Yannis Kontos (t/Athens); laif/Krause (ca/Cairo); Gamma/Eric Vandeville (t/Naples). Construction Photography.com: Xavier de Canto (t/Barcelona). Corbis: Alex Steedman (t/London). Getty Images: National Geographic/Richard Nowitz (bl); The Image Bank/Harald Sund (t/St Petersburg). Lonely Planet Images: Bradley Mayhew (ca/Shanghai). Rex Features: Henryk T. Kaiser (ca/Warsaw). Still Pictures: Ron Giling (ca/Mexico City). SuperStock: age fotostock/Gonzalo Pérez Mata (cb/Valencia); age fotostock/Bartomeu Amengual (cb/Berlin); age fotostock/Bruce Bi (ca/Beijing); age fotostock/Vin Catania (cb/Paris); age fotostock/Rudy Sulgan (cb/New York); age fotostock/Renaud Visage (cb/Barcelona). 116 NASA. 117 Science Photo Library: John Reader. 118 Alamy Images: Worldwide Picture Library/John Cleare. 119 Alamy Images: StockShot/Dave Willis (l). Corbis: Reuters/Andrew Wong (br). Impact Photos: Mark Cator (bl). 120 Lonely Planet Images: Margie Politzer (l). Chris Stowers: (r). 121 Action Plus: Steve Bardens (bc); Richard Francis (r). Alamy Images: www.gerardbrown.co.uk (c). Corbis: Larry Kasperek (r); Chris Lisle (br); Don Mason (l). Empics Ltd: AP/Tina Fineburg (tl); AP (c). Getty Images: AFP/Javier Soriano (bl); Stone/Paul Chesley (c). 128 Action Plus: Franck Faugere (r). Empics Ltd: AP/Christophe Ena (l). 129 Corbis: Tim de Waele (tr). Empics Ltd: DPA/Bernard Papon (c); AP/Alessandro Trovati (l). 130 Corbis: Jon Hicks (l). Still Pictures: Jean-Léo Dugast (c). 131 Camera Press: Gamma (bl). Empics Ltd: AP/Koji Sasahara (tc); PA/Stefan Rousseau (tl). 132 Action Plus: Glyn Kirk. Action Images: Reuters/Seth Wenig (r). 133 Action Images: Reuters/Mike Segar (r). 134 Alamy Images: Joe Tree (c). Kenny McLeish: (l). 135 Alamy Images: Buzz Pictures (tl). Camera Press: Gamma/Neema Frederic (tc/right). Masterfile: Brad Wrobleski (tr). Kenny McLeish: (tc/left). 136 Alamy Images: Chris Fredriksson (tc). Bryan and Cherry Alexander Photography: (bl). Camera Press: laif/Heuer (cr). Corbis: Flório (br). Empics Ltd: PA/Andrew Parsons (cl). Phil Orsman: (tr). 137 Corbis: Anders Ryman. 138 Adams Picture Library: Alan Moore (clb). Alamy Images: Roberto Aquilano (bl); Ian Leonard (br). Rex Features: Shout (crb). 138-139 Corbis: Patrick Bennett. 140 Alamy Images: Trevor Smithers ARPS (cra). Corbis: epa/B.K. Bangash (crb); Lester Lefkowitz (tr); Anthony Njuguna (bl); Richard T. Nowitz (br). Masterfile: Alan Davey (tl). SuperStock: age fotostock/Andre Maslennikov (cr). 141 Getty Images: The Image Bank/Thomas Schmitt. 142 Alamy Images: Kim Karpeles (r). Corbis: John H. Clark (l). Robert Haught, AllMonster.com: (t) (c) (b). 144 Corbis: Gary Kufner. 145 Alamy Images: guichaoua (bl). Corbis: Jim Zuckerman (b). Robert Harding Picture Library: Premium Stock (r). Getty Images: age fotostock/Michael S. Nolan (t). 146 Action Plus: Eric Vargiolu (ca). Getty Images: AFP/Martin Bureau (bc). Mitsubishi Motor Sports: (cb). Daniel Roeseler: (t). 146-147 Mitsubishi Motor Sports: (t/legs 1 to 16). 147 Daniel Roeseler: (br). 148 Getty Images: China Photos. 149 Getty Images: AFP/Peter Parks (cl); China Photos (l) (cr) (r). 150 Alamy Images: isifa Image Service s.r.o. (r). Orient-Express Hotels Trains & Cruises: (l). 150-151 Corbis: Carl & Ann Purcell. 151 The Blue Train: (bc). Camera Press: laif/Heuer (r). Corbis: Jeremy Horner (tc/right); Sygma/Richard Smith (br). Orient-Express Hotels Trains & Cruises: (tc/left). Rex Features: (l). 152-153 Getty Images: The Image Bank/Tomek Sikora (background). 154 Corbis: Lucidio Studio Inc. (br). 160 Action Plus: Icon SMI/Brian Cleary (l). Getty Images: Clive Mason (r). 161 Alamy Images:

Tony Watson (b). Empics Ltd: AP/Al Behrman (tr). Getty Images: AFP/Valery Hache (ca). Courtesy of McLaren Cars Limited, www.mclarencars.com: (tl). Keith Scott/rallyxpics.com: (cl). 165 Corbis: Ted Soqui (br). 166 Corbis: Sygma/David Brauchli (r). Garry Stuart (bl) (bc). 167 Alamy Images: Rod Lorance (r). Getty Images: AFP/Marcus Brandt (tc). 168 Action Images: Lee Mills (br). Alan Whale. 169 Action Plus: Richard Francis (tr). Action Images: Sporting Pictures/Simon Miles (br); Neil Tingle (bl). Alan Whale: (tl). 178-179 Corbis: zefa/Klaus Hackenberg. 180 Corbis: (4/b) (5/t). Leonard de Selva (5/b). DK Images: Courtesy of The Science Museum, London/James Stevenson (4/t). Getty Images: Hulton Archive (3/b). Science Museum, London: (1/b). 181 Aviation Picture Library: (2/t). aviation-images.com: (5/b). Camera Press: (3/t). Corbis: Bettmann (4/t). Empics Ltd: AP/Fabrice Cofferini (5/t). NASA: (3/b) (4/b); Dryden Flight Research Center (1/b). Science Photo Library: Novosti (2/b). TRH Pictures: (1/t). 182 SuperStock: Steve Vidler. 183 SuperStock: Witold Skrypczak. 184 21st Century Airships Inc.: (tr). Rex Features: Lehtikuva Oy (br). courtesy of ZLT, Zeppelin Luftschifftechnik: (bl) (tl). 185 courtesy of ZLT, Zeppelin Luftschifftechnik. 186 Getty Images: Jump Run Productions (c); Stone/Dan Smith (l). 186-187 Getty Images: Jump Run Productions. 187 Imagestate: Andy Belcher (br); Tom Sanders (cb) (tr). Rex Features: Simon Ward (ca). 188 aviation-images.com: Mark Wagner (r). Empics Ltd: AP/Rob Swanson (b). 189 AirTeamImages.com: Gary Watt (br). aviation-images.com: Mark Wagner (tr) (bl). courtesy Carter Aviation Technologies: Jason Bynum (t). 191 courtesy Gulfstream Aerospace Corporation: (t) (br). 192 aviation-images.com: Mark Wagner (r). 192-193 Alamy Images: Mark Hamilton. 193 Courtesy of U.S. Air Force: (r). 194-195 Denis Glikman, http://www.la-grange-numerique.com. 198 Airbus: (t) (r). Airbus-image exm company: P. Masele (b). aviation-images.com: (cl). 199 Airbus: (tr); Airbus-image exm company: H. Gousse (b). 208 SuperStock: Pixoi Ltd (bl/background) (t/background). 209 SuperStock: Pixoi Ltd (background). 210 Aviation Picture Library: (bc). Corbis: George Hall (c). Jim Green: (l). courtesy, SAS Group: (tc). 210-211 The Advertising Archives: (t) (c) (b). 211 The Advertising Archives: (tl) (cl) (clb) (c). courtesy, Air France: (tr) (crb). Corbis: Dean Conger (br). 212 Photo by Gate Gourmet: (tr) (br). Sophia Tampakopoulos-Turner: (l). 213 aviation-images.com: Mark Wagner (bc). The Flight Collection: Hoare (tc); Slick Shoots (br). Photo by Gate Gourmet: (tl) (tr) (bl). 214 Oksana Badrak, Superhappybunny, www.superhappybunny.com: (5/c). David Blaiklock, www.ekaada.com.au: (3/t). Jon Burgerman, www.jonburgerman.com: (4/t). (c) Furi Furi Company: (3/c). Louise Helliwell, www.louisehelliwell.com: (4/c). Syl Hillier, www.tapetentier.de: (1/c). Patrick Padeau, www.charade-design. com: (2/c). Frederick Sanchez, FFred, www.ffred.net: (6/c). Mark Suppelsa, seventy7.ca: (1/t). Morgan Thomas, www.bwoup.com: (2/t). http://www.vonster.com: (r). 215 Airsicknessbags.com: (all). 216 Reproduced with kind permission of Airbus UK: L. Baynes (b). Rex Features: David Hodges (t). 217 AirTeamImages.com: Belpix (tl). Camera Press: Gamma/De Malgaive (bl). NASA: Dryden Flight Research Center/Tony Landis (b). 225 Camera Press: Gamma/Photo News/Tanguy Jockmans (r). 226 Corbis: Reuters/Sergei Karpukhin (l). Getty Images: Scaled Composites (r). Starchaser Industries Limited, www.starchaser.co.uk: (c). 226-227 Getty Images: The Image Bank/Kevin Kelley (background). 227 aviation-images.com: (r). Empics Ltd: AP/HO/The Space Island Group (tr). Space Adventures, Ltd: (bl). courtesy Virgin Galactic: (br). 228 aviation-images.com: Mark Wagner. 229 aviation-images.com: Mark Wagner (t). NASA: (c) (b). 230-231 Getty Images: The Image Bank/Color Day Production. 232 Rex Features: Sipa Press (t). Jay Wade: (b). 232-233 Courtesy of Advanced Transport Systems Ltd. 233 Alamy Images: Joseph Szurszewski (br). Rex Features: (b); Sipa Press (bl). 234 Getty Images: AFP/Damien Meyer (4/b). 235 Alamy Images: sdbphoto.com (1/b). Corbis: Courtesy of Ducati: (10/b). 236-237 SuperStock: age fotostock/Frank Lukasseck (r). 238-239 SuperStock: age fotostock/Frank Lukasseck (r). 240 Getty Images: Stone/Glen Allison (t).

Jacket images: Front: Getty Images: Stone cb; Masterfile: Forest Johnson bc; NASA: NASA Langley Research Center (NASA-LaRC) tc. Spine: Getty Images: Brand X Pictures; Front Endpapers: Getty Images: Kim Sayer; Back Endpapers: Getty Images: The Image Bank/Pete Turner.

All other images © Dorling Kindersley
For further information see: www.dkimages.com